Social Work in Education and Children's Services

Transforming Social Work Practice – titles in the series

To order, please contact our distributor: BEBC Distribution, Albion Close, Parkstone, Poole, BH12 3LL. Telephone: 0845 230 9000, email: **learningmatters@bebc.co.uk**. You can also find more information on each of these titles and our other learning resources at www.learningmatters.co.uk.

Social Work in Education and Children's Services

NIGEL HORNER AND STEVE KRAWCZYK

Series Editors: Jonathan Parker and Greta Bradley

LearningMatters

SP
MT

First published in 2006 by Learning Matters Ltd.

British Library Cataloguing in Publication Data
A CIP record for this book is available from the British Library.

ISBN-10: 1 84445 045 7
ISBN-13: 978 1 84445 045 9

Cover and text design by Code 5 Design Associates Ltd
Project management by Deer Park Productions
Typeset by Pantek Arts Ltd, Maidstone, Kent
Printed and bound in Great Britain by Bell & Bain Ltd, Glasgow

Learning Matters Ltd
33 Southernhay East
Exeter EX1 1NX
Tel: 01392 215560
Email: *info@learningmatters.co.uk*
www.learningmatters.co.uk

12/19/06

Contents

Dedications

From Nigel: For my mother, Biddy Horner, who has demonstrated such resilience and adaptability – at any age!

From Steve: For Maree, John and Paul, who ask for so little, yet deserve so much more.

Acknowledgements

The authors would like to express their appreciation to members of the East Midlands Education Welfare Consortium, and to Tony Stevens and Linda Kelly for providing case examples.

We wish to express our particular appreciation to George Gilmore, Head Teacher of Applefields School in the City of York, for invaluable advice and information regarding children with additional needs.

Introduction

What a wise parent would desire for his (sic) own children, so a nation, in so far as it is wise, must desire for all children.
(R.H. Tawney, 1931, p146, quoting the Board of Education, 1931, pxxix)

ACHIEVING A SOCIAL WORK DEGREE

This chapter will help you the meet the following National Occupational Standards (TOPSS, 2002):
Key Role 1: Prepare for and work with individuals, families, carers, groups and communities to assess their needs and circumstances:
- Prepare for social work contact and involvement.

Key Role 5: Manage and be accountable, with supervision and support, for your own social work practice within your organisation.
- Work within multi-disciplinary and multi-organisational teams, networks and systems.

Key Role 6: Demonstrate professional competence in social work practice:
- Research, analyse, evaluate and use current knowledge of best social work practice.
- Contribute to the promotion of best social work practice.

It will also introduce you to the following academic standards as set out in the social work subject benchmark statement (Quality Assurance Agency for Higher Education (QAA), 2000):

2.2.1 Defining principles
Social work is located within different social welfare contexts. Within the UK there are different traditions of social welfare (influenced by legislation, historical development and social attitudes) and these have shaped both social work education and practice in community-based settings including group care.

2.2.2 Defining principles
There are competing views in society at large on the nature of social work and its place and purpose. Social work practice and education inevitably reflect these differing perspectives on the role of social work in relation to social justice, social care and social order.

3.1.2 The service delivery context
The significance of inter-relationships with other social services, especially education, housing, health, income maintenance and criminal justice.

3.1.5 The nature of social work practice
The factors and processes that facilitate effective inter-disciplinary, inter-professional and inter-agency collaboration and partnership.

Setting the scene: Children, young people, families and education

In 2003 there were 11.7 million children under the age of 16 in the UK (*SocietyGuardian*, 2005) which represents a relatively consistent figure over the past 30 years, although we are now in a period of actual decline, and the total is projected to fall to 11.1 million by 2011. As life expectancy continues to rise, then the proportion of the population defined as children or young people will decrease to the point where it is estimated that by 2013, the number of people over 65 will, for the first time ever, exceed those aged under 16. This amounts to a seismic shift in the nation's demography, and will have significant implications in terms of the importance of education and training as the base camp from which children and young people will navigate their lengthening working lives in pursuit of an ever more elusive and unpredictable goal of financial security in old age.

However, this book is not about adult working life – now called the Second Age – nor the expanding and lengthening post-working period of life – the Third Age – but it is about a core part of the beginning of the life course, namely the activities and experiences in the First Age, in childhood and adolescence. It is about education and schooling, and its importance and meaning for children, young people and their families and carers.

For the majority of children and young people, schooling amounts to a mixed blessing of encouragements and disappointments, of challenges and successes, of friendships made and sustained or made and lost, of teachers liked and admired or disliked and feared, of lasting memories which are, for the majority, mostly positive. That said, for a small but significant number of children and young people, school amounts to little less than a place of oppression, violence, fear, failure, rejection, exclusion and despair. Indeed, for yet another sub-group, schooling is primarily something to be avoided altogether. For particularly vulnerable groups, such as disabled children or those looked after by the local authority, *good* schooling can play a particularly significant role in assisting and promoting their resilience and in developing their potential, whilst *poor* schooling can set them back significantly. Sonia Jackson, who since the 1980s has studied the educational outcomes for children and young people in public care, affirms that:

> ... *education is the aspect of children's lives where it is most essential to preserve continuity, in relationships with teachers and friends, attendance at lessons, keeping up with curriculum content, and ensuring understanding of important elements of each subject.*
> (Jackson, 2002, p46)

In other words, *schooling matters*, and this book is principally focused on those vulnerable groups of pupils for whom the inclusive or exclusive tenor of their schooling makes such a lasting difference. Furthermore, young people's experience of schooling may have significant consequences in terms of the unfolding of their life course. The poor educational achievement record for so many adults subsequently incarcerated within the secure criminal justice system serves to underscore and reinforce the assertion by Herbert that:

Mass formal education has created serious problems for the life goals of adolescents with educational difficulties. For academically successful adolescents, school is a bridge between the world of childhood and world of adulthood. For children unwilling or unable to learn, school is a place where the battle against society is likely to begin.
(Herbert, 2002, p362)

School matters most for those most excluded from society

This book is not primarily about an education process that works successfully, one so often based upon a positive and mutually supportive triangular dynamic of parent(s), child and school. (Such a book might more appropriately appear in a mainstream educational series.) As part of the *Transforming Social Work Practice* series, and thus being primarily concerned with the business of social work and social care, this book is about that small but very significant number of children and young people for whom schooling is potentially or actually difficult – whether that difficulty flows from their experiences of a disabling society (Oliver, 1996), from a discriminatory school environment, from adverse family circumstances, or from their experience of being looked after by the local authority. Such children and young people are most likely to be involved in the specialist or targeted services staffed by various professions including social workers.

It is worth noting how unlikely it is that this book would have been written until recently, even as late as the end of the twentieth century. Whilst a few determined social work and educational academic researchers (such as Fletcher-Campbell and Hall, 1990; Jackson, 1994 and 2002; Jackson and Sanchev, 2001) had been paying much needed attention to the educational under-achievements of children and young people looked after in public care – and thereby significantly influencing and shaping the setting of qualifications targets for children in public care as part of the Quality Protects programme (Department of Health, 1998a) – the actual relationship between the professional activities of teaching and social work had been largely ignored. (A notable exception is the innovative text *Childcare services and the teacher*, written by Katrin Fitzherbert in 1977). In the last decade however, there has emerged a far-reaching and fundamental examination of the sociological phenomena known as *The School* itself, its social role and function, and this has been connected to the political imperatives to address the structural consequences (such as anti-social behaviour and youth offending) that are allegedly associated with school disaffection, underachievement and non-school attendance. This has lead to the current policy objective to transform and reframe the historically fragmented relationship between education and social work.

The 1997 election mantra of Tony Blair, leader of the New Labour Party, *Education, Education, Education*, was not just about class sizes, teacher performance, league tables and examination results, although it was stated that:

... the first priority of a new government must be to raise general educational standards ... New Labour believes that, through schooling, standards are more important than structures ... Under a New Labour government, there will be zero tolerance of failure.
(Mandelson and Liddle, 1996, p92)

xi

What is of particular significance for those working at the social work and education interface is the manifest conviction held by the Labour Government about the importance of education in terms of addressing broader social issues that lie beyond the specifics of targeted school performance, as exemplified by Tony Blair's conviction that *(I)t is great for the individual, it is right for society and it is also economically essential* (Tony Blair, in the *Times Educational Supplement*, 5 July 2002). Indeed, the importance of school achievement has been repeatedly affirmed by the officially held belief in the transformative potential of education in relation to another of the original *New Labour Five Pledges*, namely tackling youth offending:

> *Truancy is a growing problem in many areas, notably the inner cities. Some classes are depleted by 20 or 30 per cent because of truanting. What are truant children doing? They are up to mischief or worse.*
> (Blair, 1996, p239)

Such sentiments were indeed echoed and amplified in the Social Exclusion Unit's report on *Truancy and School Exclusion*:

> *Truancy and exclusions have reached a crisis point. The thousands of children who are not in school on most schooldays have become a significant cause of crime. Many of today's non-attenders are in danger of becoming tomorrow's criminals and unemployed. No-one knows precisely how many children are out of school at any time because of truancy or exclusion. But each year at least one million children play truant, and over 100,000 children are excluded temporarily. Some 13,000 are excluded permanently.*
> (*Truancy and School Exclusion*, report by the Social Exclusion Unit, May 1998) p3

In fact, this alleged association between non-school attendance and crime would appear to be supported by a range of evidence. Truants are indeed three times as likely to offend as non-truants and half of school-age offenders have been excluded from school (Graham and Bowling, 1995, reiterated in the *Guardian*, 2003). As a result, the perceived core business for the education welfare service, that of addressing truancy, has been reaffirmed as a high priority for the government since its accession to power in 1997. The Government's Social Exclusion Unit report *Bridging the Gap* (Social Exclusion Unit, 1999) highlighted the links between poor attendance, disaffection, poor behaviour and impaired life chances, and later studies have repeatedly linked school absence with higher levels of teenage pregnancy, youth offending and drug and alcohol abuse (*SocietyGuardian*, 2005, p93). Furthermore, Jackson and McParlin (2006, p90) cite evidence from the British Cohort Studies, which:

> *shows that the quality of adult life is closely related to educational qualifications. Each step up the educational ladder is associated with improvements in health, both mental and physical, employment, housing, family life, absence of addiction problems and lower risk of involvement with the criminal justice system.*
> (Jackson and Simon, 2005)

What is more revealing is that the greatest benefits are to be found at the *top end* of the educational ladder, and that entry into higher education results in explicit gains in terms of financial, emotional and health security. Or, to put this presumed causal relationship another way: *education attainment at 16 (is) the most important predictor of future participation in learning and of labour market prospects* (Pearce and Hillman, 1998, p7).

As a result of this *evidence*, the Government set out an ambitious and heavily funded agenda to tackle the impact of *disengagement*. This New Labour thesis is essentially a reiteration of long held ideas, traditionally associated with the Conservative Party. As Maitles notes (2002, p73), Dr Rhodes Boyson listed his concerns about education as long ago as his 1975 publication, with the following chapter heading: *Signs of Breakdown: Illiteracy, Violence and Indiscipline, Truancy, Collapse of Confidence* (Boyson, 1975, pp1–2). Whilst such views were anathema to the traditional democratic and socialist left at the time, they have within the space of 30 years migrated from what was then seen as the right wing of Conservatism to become the accepted middle ground orthodoxy, albeit with a different spin, but now rooted in the language of diversity, inclusion, stakeholding and citizenship.

At the heart of the modernising *joined up* project for education, child health and social services (see Chapter 2) is an axiomatic yet unstated conviction that the residual functions of the latter structure's profession – namely, social work tasks – are indeed vital, but they should become progressively unnecessary as the enhancing, promoting and protecting benefits of a *good* education, underpinned by improving health, are available to all, not just the few. Such assumptions are not without their critics. Thrupp (1999, p182) notes: *We should bear in mind that being optimistic about school reform has helped avoid dealing with tough questions about the impact on education of social inequalities of power and resources*. In other words, the idea that standards can be inexorably raised through the pursuit of a heady mix of policy, legislation, targets, initiatives, school improvement plans, inspections and reviews, all serves to divert attention away from the underlying and deep rooted and indeed broadening social inequalities and divisions within communities and society.

Although the incoming New Labour Government published its review of the social work profession under the title of *Modernising Social Services* (Department of Health, 1998b), there has been an absence, subsequently, of public utterances of the social *services* term, in tandem with, however, a reinforcement of the concepts of social *care*, social *work* and social *workers*. Accordingly, the Care Standards Act of 2000 defined *Social Worker* as a protected title, established the process whereby social workers would be trained, registered and de- registered, and provided a Code of Conduct for those engaged in both social care and social work. Thus, whilst social *work* as an activity has been further professionalised and regulated, the old certainties as to its historic practice base – local authority *social services* departments as configured since the Local Authority Social Services Act of 1970 that ensued from the Seebohm Committee Report of 1968 – have progressively withered in the face of the deluge of New Labour *Welfare* restructurings (for a further discussion of these developments, see Horner, 2006).

It is not the purpose of this book to consider and explore the emerging realignments between health, social work and other agencies that are taking place in relation to adult care services (see Department of Health, 2005). However, following the passing of the Children Act 2004, it has been a requirement for each local authority to establish directorates of children's services, thereby completing the transfer of all social work concerned with children and young people and families from the control of the Department of Health into the arms of the Department for Education and Skills (DfES) (this began in 2003).

This represents a significant change in professional culture and associated structures. In 1994, Sonia Jackson (who, as stated above, has been at the forefront of researching and addressing the educational needs of children within the looked after (care) system) noted the *deep split between education and care which runs through all our institutions and service for children* (Jackson, 1994, p273), and Gilligan (1998, p13) similarly observed that *schools seem remarkably invisible in the field of child and family social work* and furthermore stated that *(T)he role of the teacher as the professional with most contact with children seems to go virtually unacknowledged in much of social work and wider welfare circles.*

So, much has changed in the last decade. No longer can *social work* and *education* operate along parallel lines. The two defined professional roles – that of *social worker* and *teacher* – have been progressively led into an arranged marriage, with the children's services department being designated as their *ideal home*. However, this is to be *home* to a complex and inclusive family group, which will also embrace education welfare workers, Special Educational Needs Co-ordinators, Connexions Personal Advisers, learning mentors, health visitors and midwives, child and adolescent mental health service staff, and possibly youth offending teams. To continue the domestic metaphor, if the new family is to get along, and to be effective for service users, then it is essential that parties understand each others' roles, duties and responsibilities. It is precisely our interest in these arrangements that has prompted this book to be written.

The purpose of the book

In the light of the profound changes that are confronting the child welfare landscape, it is essential that all practitioners working with children, young people and families have an understanding of the current and anticipated inter-relationship between social work and education, and with other professional groupings. Historically, some aspects of social work practice – such as education welfare, child and adolescent mental health services and services for children with disabilities – have worked within or alongside an education framework, whilst other areas have been less engaged, or have indeed been decidedly disengaged. Nevertheless, the current Government's conviction about the importance of education *per se* has resulted in a fundamental realignment of relationships within central government, which will have an impact upon all levels of practice (mostly notably the transfer of overall responsibility for childcare social work services from the Department of Health to the DfES). Consequently, it is now apparent that the education sector is at the centre of the Government's plans to address the universal needs and well-being of children and young people.

The Children Act 2004 requires the creation of multi-agency frameworks, children's services with trust-like arrangements and information sharing networks over the next five years, all to be overseen by the Children's Commissioner. According to Margaret Hodge, the erstwhile Minister for Children, *the government's five-year strategy for children and learners reaffirms our commitment to high-quality childcare for all, giving children a good start in life, and supporting parents in their choices.*

Such a strategy will require new ways of working in education, in social work, in education welfare and in the emerging professional roles that will be created to straddle and bridge traditional service domains. Accordingly, we hope the following material will be useful and interesting to a range of people, particularly those undertaking qualifying courses with the intention of joining the broadening children's workforce. Furthermore, we hope the book will be of value to current employees and practitioners, who might gain some understanding of the roles, responsibilities, duties and practices of their new colleagues.

Who is this book for?

We hope this book will be of interest and hopefully value to the following:

- students undertaking qualifying social work degrees;

- those planning to enter the education welfare, Connexions, learning mentors and youth offending services;

- those already practising in such services;

- professionals engaged in education, including staff in pupil referral units, Special Educational Needs Co-ordinators (SENCOs), Education Liaison Co-ordinators and those charged with developing full service extended schools programmes;

- workers in youth offending teams, youth services, Connexions, learning mentors, children's trusts and other services for children, young people and their families;

- practitioners whose roles broadly fall under the auspices of the term the children's workforce.

Indeed, as the Teacher Training Agency (TTA) states (2005, p13, as cited in Quinney, 2006, p79) teachers must be able to demonstrate:

Understanding of the distinct roles and responsibilities of other professionals including, for example, social workers, educational psychologists, education welfare officers, youth justice workers, Early Years or play workers, school nurses or other health professionals.
(TTA, 2005, p13)

It is in the context of this requirement that this book aims to make a contribution.

The series context

This series of *Learning Matters* books have been developed to support the learning of students undertaking a social work degree, in accordance with The Requirements for Social Work Training (2002). The advent of the new award for qualification in social work forms one part of a raft of major developments in the institutional structures that define, regulate and lead social work, and it is important for you, the student, to consider why these elements of the Modernising Social Services Agenda (Department of Health, 1998) have come to be seen as necessary.

The context of the National Occupational Standards – social work and support services for children and young people – and the QAA benchmark statement for social work

It is anticipated that a number of readers of this book will be undertaking the social work degree in higher education settings. With this in mind, the material and associated exercises have been designed to help you to meet the Department of Health requirements for the new degree in social work.

In addition to the social work degree requirements, the government has defined core competences for the broad childcare workforce (DfES, 2004) to include those working in children's trusts, in daycare settings, in education welfare services, in youth justice, and is beginning to develop an integrated qualifications framework for the children's workforce. It is intended and hoped that this book will be of value and interest to those studying for allied qualifications beyond teacher training and social work.

Furthermore, the book will assist you in meeting elements of the academic subject benchmarks for social work (QAA, 2000), and each chapter identifies the elements of the benchmark statement that are to be addressed.

In summary, as with other texts in the *Learning Matters* series (*Transforming Social Work Practice*), this book will link to the Requirements for Social Work Education, as defined by:

- new degree regulations (GSCC, 2000);

- requirements as defined by the Department of Health (2000);

- National Occupational Standards (TOPSS (now Skills for Care) 2000);

- QAA benchmark statement for social work (QAA, 2000).

An overview of the chapters

In **Chapter 1**, we will consider historical perspectives on **Schools, Social Work and Education Welfare**, including the history of compulsory education, the emergence of school attendance enforcement, the rise and fall of segregated special education, and the development of school inclusion policies and practices for children with special needs. An overview of the historical phases of both education and social work developments will enable you to have an understanding of the nature of the contemporary social work task in relation to working with children, young people and families. In turn, you will be able to reflect upon the required knowledge, skills and values deemed necessary for the modern social *worker* to be able to carry out the modern social *work* role.

In **Chapter 2**, we will consider and reflect upon understanding **The Children Act 2004**, which is anticipated to form the cornerstone for the reorganisation of services to children, young people and their families. Government policy concerning the redefinition of the role of the school as part of community regeneration will also be explored.

In **Chapter 3** we will look at the **Broader Legal Context of Contemporary Practice** including aspects of the Children Act 1989, the Disability Discrimination Act 1995, the

Education Act 1996, the Disabled Children Act 2000, the Special Educational Needs and Disability Act 2001, the Anti-social Behaviour Act 2003, all within the context of the Children Act 2004.

In **Chapter 4** entitled **School's Out**, we will introduce and explore the ways of making sense of disaffection, absenteeism and exclusion, drawing upon theories of childhood and adolescence (such as transitions, resilience and identity, peer pressure, identity and development). Furthermore, this chapter will examine differences in terms of defined school-related 'problems' as defined by race, ethnicity grouping gender, culture and diversity.

In **Chapter 5**, we will consider contemporary education welfare/education social work practice in terms of **School's In**. This section will examine the business of education welfare provision, contemporary responses to school attendance and truancy problems, government policy targeting attendance and unauthorised absence, the impact of Audit Commission performance indicators on referrals; home visits; truancy sweeps and the numbers of prosecutions, and the role of bullying and anti-bullying strategies. Finally, children with special needs will be located within this contested area.

In **Chapter 6**, broader **Related Issues and Practice Challenges** are explored, including *Education otherwise and alternative provision*, the complex question of child employment, and a review of debates and trends concerning the education of children with disabilities or special needs.

In **Chapter 7, Eduactional outcomes and children looked after,** attention is paid to the specific educational needs of children looked after by the local authority social services/children's services department.

In **Chapter 8**, we will reflect upon **What are we going to do about it? Assessment and Intervention**. In other words, we consider the intervention options available to the practitioner. You will be introduced to assessment as a theory driven activity, to the principles of assessment, to an extended case study and then modes of intervention.

In the penultimate **Chapter 9**, we will reflect the Government's interest in **What Works?** and will explore the evidence base for effective inclusive education.

Finally, in **Chapter 10**, we will consider **Pointers to the Future** and attempt to offer some educated guesses about the shape of education and social work in coming years and decades. The chapters are followed by various Appendices (a timeline of education, an audit tool for inclusive education and useful contacts).

Learning styles

This book contains:

- links to National Occupational Standards and the benchmark statement at the beginning of each chapter;
- case studies – to demonstrate application of knowledge in practice;
- research summaries – to underpin knowledge with theory;
- activities – to check learning and encourage reflection on practice;
- further reading.

Consistent with the other titles in the *Transforming Social Work Practice* series, this book is designed to be interactive. You are encouraged to work through the book as an active participant, taking responsibility for your learning, in order to increase your knowledge, understanding and ability to apply this learning to practice. You will be expected to reflect creatively on how your immediate learning needs can be met in the area of understanding social work within a broad context and how your professional learning can be developed in your future career.

Case studies throughout the book will help you to examine theories and models for social work and education welfare practice. We have devised activities that require you to reflect on experiences, situations and events and help you to review and summarise learning undertaken. In this way your knowledge will become deeply embedded as part of your development. When you come to undertake practice-learning opportunities in an agency, the work and reflection undertaken here will help you to improve and hone your skills and knowledge.

Introduction to case studies

The case studies used are based upon actual service users, although their identities have been disguised. In drawing upon characters that represent different ethnic groups and cultures, it is intended that the reader will identify both the common issues and those that are specific to working in an ethnically and culturally sensitive manner with different communities, traditions and beliefs. An essential requirement for achieving competence in social work practice is to value difference, and to work in a manner that respects different cultures, faiths, beliefs and traditions. Such a values perspective needs, therefore, to be applied to all of the case examples in the following text.

Case study: Brett

Brett comes from a white family with Scottish roots. He is 9 years of age, a Year 5 pupil who seems to enjoy school, but who rarely attends, and is frequently late. At school, his over-exuberant and attention seeking behaviours and poorly developed social skills are coupled with significant under-achievement and this is generating concern amongst his teachers.

Case study: Danielle

Danielle is a 14-year-old white girl, in Year 10. Since the beginning of the academic year her school attendance has deteriorated to less than 25 per cent from its previously satisfactory level. Now six months into her GCSE course, she is significantly behind with her work, homework is rarely submitted and attempts by the school to support Danielle have failed. She has now refused to attend at all, saying that school *does her head in* and that staff routinely pick on her. Her case is the subject of a discussion between the school teachers and the education welfare service.

Case study: Joshua

Joshua is a Year 7 pupil from a white family. He has started his second term in the manner he ended the first, with a fixed-term exclusion for hitting and swearing at a member of staff. He is unable to get through a full lesson without causing disruption or leaving the room. Other concerns include poor attendance and punctuality, an inability to complete class work and homework and a level of social skills that prevents him forming and sustaining peer relationships.

Case study: Chantelle

Chantelle is a black British young woman, in Year 11, with just two terms to complete before her GCSE exams. She is a *looked after* young person, under section 20 of the Children Act 1989, and is resident in a foster home. Her school has been severely disrupted by frequent moves and changes over the past five years, but she is committed to taking her exams. Her personal education plan is being reviewed.

Case study: Sarbjit

Sarbjit is a British born Sikh now aged 11, and in Year 6 at her special school. She has been defined as having a mild learning disability, caused by birth complications.

Case study: Jim

Jim is a 15-year-old, Year 11 pupil whose family is rooted in the Romany tradition. He has attended very little at school over the past few months, and is often not to be found at home. He sleeps at various locations around the town and mixes with older young people. He is known to be using various substances, such as heroin and amphetamines. His situation is of concern to various agencies, including the police, the youth offending team and the education welfare service.

Case study: Rebecca

Rebecca, a Year 5 pupil in a mainstream primary school, has experienced difficulties throughout her school career and finds it hard to cope with many aspects of school. She has poor relationships with her peers, needs additional support with the curriculum and presents a range of challenging behaviours that disrupts her learning and that of her peers.

Case study: Jose

A call is received from a neighbour about Jose who is believed to be about 14 years of age, from a Portuguese family, and who does not appear to be attending school. Details are taken and the education welfare officer visits the family home to be told by the mother, who is only able to speak a few words of English, that Jose does not want to go to school and that he is perfectly happy working with his father and brothers at a vegetable and fruit packaging company 15 miles away.

Case study: Winston

Winston, a 14-year-old young person of Afro-Caribbean descent, has been made the subject of an Emergency Protection Order following a major family breakdown during which his father was remanded in custody and his mother left the family home, destination unknown. Winston has been placed with the only available foster family who live some 35 miles from Winston's own home and from his previous school.

Case study: Adam

Adam is a 10-year-old white child. He lives with his three brothers and his biological parents, who are both heroin users. Apart from his sporadic school attendance, there are significant concerns about his poor social skills, his chaotic behaviour, his risk of offending and his general safety.

C H A P T E R   S U M M A R Y

The primary objective of this book is to prepare you – the student, the newly qualified social worker, the teacher, the education support worker, the education welfare officer – for effective practice in the *brave new world* of integrate children's services. This is new territory for everyone: it is not a return to the pre-Seebohm children's departments, but represents a realignment of the relationships within and between professional groups engaged in child welfare in its broadest sense. We hope the book will promote improved outcomes for children, young people, their families and carers by enabling you to engage in informed practice and to make a contribution to shaping modern integrated services.

Furthermore, this book is about your learning and reflection – as students or as practitioners – and we hope you will engage with it freely and willingly, and that it may make a small contribution to your *real* education. As Ezra Pound observed in the *ABC of reading* (1934): *Real education must ultimately be limited to one who INSISTS on knowing, the rest is mere sheep-herding*.

Chapter 1

Schools, social work and education welfare: Historical perspectives

Ignorance is like a delicate exotic fruit, touch it and the bloom is gone. The whole theory of modern education is radically unsound. Fortunately, in England, at any rate, education produces no effect whatsoever.
(Oscar Wilde, *The Importance of Being Earnest*, 1895, Act 1)

… what we must look for here is, first, religious and moral principle; secondly, gentlemanly conduct; third, intellectual ability.
(Dr Thomas Arnold, Headmaster of Rugby School (cited in Strachey, 1986, p167))

We've got compulsory education, which is a responsibility of hideous importance; and we tyrannise children to do that which they don't want, and we don't produce results.
(Sir Keith Joseph (quoted in Chitty 1997, p80))

A C H I E V I N G   A   S O C I A L   W O R K   D E G R E E

This chapter will help you to meet the following National Occupational Standards:
Key Role 1: Prepare for and work with individuals, families, carers, groups and communities to assess their needs and circumstances:
- Prepare for social work contact and involvement.

It will also introduce you to the following academic standards as set out in the social work subject benchmark statement (Quality Assurance Agency for Higher Education (QAA), 2000):

2.2.1 Defining principles
Social work is located within different social welfare contexts. Within the UK there are different traditions of social welfare (influenced by legislation, historical development and social attitudes) and these have shaped both social work education and practice in community-based settings including group care.

3.1.2 The service delivery context
- The location of contemporary social work within both historical and comparative perspectives.
- The complex relationships between public, social and political philosophies, policies and priorities and the organisation and practice of social work, including the contested nature of these.

3.1.3 Values and ethics
- The nature, historical evolution and application of social work values.
- Rights, responses, freedom, authority and power in the practice of social workers as moral and statutory agents.

3.1.5 The nature of social work practice
- The factors and processes that facilitate effective inter-disciplinary, inter-professional and inter-agency collaboration and partnership.

A very brief history of education

The dramatist Oscar Wilde held a particular view of education – as something necessarily damaging and brutal in its destruction of presumed innocence/ignorance – which is at once amusing and yet striking by virtue of being so out of step with the views and beliefs of the times in which it was said (and indeed with today's *received ideas*). We have learned to take it for granted that education is *a good thing*, and that therefore all that matters is making *good education* available for all. But like any aspect of childhood, modern ideas about education are socially and historically constructed, and are therefore contested and complex. Whilst the State invests significant resources into trying to ensure and enforce school attendance for all children and young people between the ages of 5 and 16, such efforts are driven, in historical terms, by relatively recent ideas about the desirability of universal mass education. After all, the upper classes in sixteenth- and seventeenth-century England were in fear of the consequences of having a readily available printed and translated Bible *and* a literate working class, both of which, they believed, would lead to a breakdown in law and the social order. They were therefore set against the idea of extending education to the populace as a whole, and thought of it as essentially a preserve of a privileged elite. Bernard Mandeville, in his 1742 work *The fable of the bees*, represents beautifully the persistence of these views:

> *The Welfare and Felicity … of every State and Kingdom require that the Knowledge of the Working Poor should be confined within the Verge of their Occupations, and never extended (as to things visible) beyond what relates to their Calling.*
> (Mandeville, 1970, pp294–95)

Yet a proportion of parents of all classes sought an education for their children, in the face of apparent resistance from children themselves. Nearly 300 years before the advent of compulsory elementary education in Britain, Shakespeare is alluding to a universal and timeless truth, that of parents making children go to school against their wishes:

> *And then the whining school-boy, with his satchel*
> *And shining morning face, creeping like a snail*
> *Unwillingly to school*
> (William Shakespeare, *As you like it*, II.vii.139)

So, it is abundantly clear that for centuries, parents, carers and families *chose* to educate their children – either at home or in formal institutions, sometimes known as schools, academies or seminaries – long before the State began to introduce the idea of compulsion. What was their motivation?

ACTIVITY **1.1**

*How do we make sense of this desire for education, for schooling, and why did post-Renaissance Europe slowly but gradually move towards universal elementary education for children? On the basis of what you have read so far, and by reflecting upon your own assumptions about education, note down **three** key reasons for this development.*

(1)

(2)

(3)

Comment

Your thoughts might have covered a number of possible motivations, which can be clustered around some general ideas:

- you might have felt that parents wanted their children to be educated in order for them to be disciplined and controlled;

- in a connected vein, you might have focused on the moral instruction of children in terms of religious understanding and adherence;

- or you might have emphasised the presumed social and economic advantage that stems from education, associated with the acquisition of manners and an understanding of arts, music and culture;

- or lastly, education might be seen as being about snobbery value, about competitive edge, about status and social advantage.

In his historical study of childhood, Cunningham (1995, pp101–102) suggests that parents had three primary motivations for sending their children to some kind of schooling:

(1) religious instruction;

(2) for the social advancement that flowed from literacy; and

(3) as a convenient childcare service.

For the majority of the population, school fees were an impediment to consistent and long-term attendance, and school numbers were clearly affected by seasonal activity (such as harvesting), temporary hardship or economic slumps. Nevertheless, as Cunningham further notes (1995, p105), numerous studies revealed the extent to which schooling originated from parental (if not child) demand, in spite of these apparent difficulties. To fully understand the emergence of mass (if not compulsory) education, we need to reflect upon the set of ideas that flowed from the Reformation, and thence from the Enlightenment in Europe.

To the Protestant leader, Martin Luther (1530), education was so important that failures in parental duty in this matter merited the intervention of others to secure the welfare of the child. He suggested that if parents did not attend to education, the *children cease to belong to their parents and fall to the care of God and community*. Such a remark presages much later beliefs by the likes of Dr Barnardo that children should be properly rescued from parents who failed to nurture, protect and educate their offspring, and which coalesced into a coherent child welfare perspective defined by Fox Harding (1997) as *Child Rescue* and *State Paternalism*.

Cunningham's study (1998) shows that compulsory education occurred in much of Europe for decades, and in some cases centuries, earlier than in England and Wales – in the seventeenth century in Scotland (in 1616, an Act of the Scottish Parliament stated that every parish should have a school and a teacher), in the eighteenth century in Saxony (1769), in Austria (1774), followed by Poland, Prussia, Hungary, France, and in the first decades of the nineteenth century in Denmark and the Netherlands.

Following on from Luther, the conviction as to the importance of education was central to the leaders of the French Revolution, with Danton stating that *children belong to society before they belong to their family* and Robespierre asserting that *the country has the right to raise its children; it should not entrust this to the pride of families or to the prejudices of particular individuals* – both quotations affirming education as the vehicle by which the State assumed the right to nurture, develop, discipline, shape, mould and indeed create its own future citizens.

In spite of the collapse of revolutionary republican ideas in France and the return of monarchy, Cunningham (1995, p156) suggests that in that country *the vast majority of children did attend a school before the 1880s … because their parents and communities wanted and expected them to, rather than because central government tried to enforce attendance*.

The very fact that education seemed more advanced in many of those European countries embroiled in the year of revolutions (1848) fed precisely into a cautious English consciousness highly resistant to State interference, and one that believed that literacy would lead to dissatisfaction, unrest and social disintegration.

Nevertheless, the demand for a literate workforce flowed from advanced industrialised capitalism, and what became established as compulsory elementary schooling was not a direct descendant of Renaissance educational philosophy, but predicated on a form of training, that was concerned with discipline, obedience, conformity, respect, punctuality and preparation for work. As the British sociologist Herbert Spencer suggested: *Education has for its object the formation of character* (*Social Statistics* I, Ch, 2.4), and the character to be formed was one rooted in the prevailing social order of industry and empire. As Parton (2006, p13) observes, the emergence of the *sciences of man* (as distinct from the sciences of material things) resulted in the school, the hospital and the prison being established as sites for both *individualising and totalising forms of knowledge*, and for developing judgments about *what is normal*. One such notion of *normalcy* has become the idea that all children over a particular age (usually five) should be formally educated, usually at school, under a scheme increasingly referred to as National Education.

In the introduction to this book, we explored the broad and optimistic vision of the New Labour project as to the benefits that are seen to inexorably accrue from raising school standards and achievement levels. Whilst the language may be different, the sentiments are direct descendants of those at the beginning of the nineteenth century:

National education is the first thing necessary. Lay but this foundation and the superstructure of prosperity and happiness, which may be erected, will rest upon a rock; lay but this foundation, poverty will be diminished and want will disappear in proportion as the lower classes are instructed in their duties for then only will they understand their true interests.
(*The Quarterly Review* VIII, 1812, cited in Petrie, 2003, p67)

Such a statement merits analysis, in that it asserts the following sequence of logically connected assertions, all of which can be translated into a set of equally inter-connected assumptions as to the value of education today:

- the poor need to be educated – through national education – as to their *duties*;

- the poor will relish education once they realise it is in their interests to be educated;

- as a result of being educated, they will be better workers and more self-reliant, and thus the pool of surplus labour, the underclass, will reduce;

- consequently, the burden of the Poor Law will diminish, leading to greater wealth creation and prosperity for all; and

- the State should invest now – by creating a system of National Education – that will produce a saving in the longer term.

Petrie (2003, p76) observes, in terms of government thinking, that *much anti-poverty policy can be seen in terms of social pedagogy*, based upon the idea that *if 'Ignorance' is reduced, then 'Want' (unemployment, social exclusion, ill-health and anti-social behaviour) will also be reduced*, and that such beliefs do indeed have a long history.

There were critics of the National Education project – notably by writers such as William Godwin, who asserted that *the project of National Education ought uniformly to be discouraged, on account of its obvious alliance with national government* (Godwin, 1793) – in other words, mass education is the means by which centralised government controls its population. But this was a minority view, and the march towards mass education held sway.

Whilst it took over 50 years for such ideas to be translated into legislation, the arguments contained within the set of premises have had currency ever since. Our concern here is with the emergence of the mandate upon local government to provide schools – and upon parents to ensure their children attended.

The emergence of compulsory education

The advent of compulsory elementary schooling marks the watershed in the creation of a social constructed childhood – which removes children from the workplace, from the adult world, and defines children in terms of economic dependency (Gittins, 1998, p57).

It was with the Education Act of 1870, also known as Forster's Education Act, that we have the real birth of the modern system of education in England. This not only gave rise to a national system of State education, but also assured the existence of a dual system within Britain of voluntary denominational (church or faith) schools sitting alongside non-denominational State schools.

The 1870 Act required the establishment of elementary schools nationwide. These were not to replace or duplicate what already existed, but to supplement those already run by the churches, by private individuals and by guilds. Therefore, the country of England was divided into school districts and in those areas where there was inadequate provision, then school boards were to be elected. These were responsible for raising sufficient funds to maintain the schools, and such establishments were often called *board schools*.

Significantly, these elementary schools had to be non-denominational (an interesting point, given the current Government's willingness to fund faith-based schools, and as distinct from the French Government's historic and continued adherence to the principles of secular education). The school boards could charge a weekly fee not exceeding nine pence, and for a limited period the boards could pay the fees if the parents were unable to do so. The voluntary schools could also receive such payment of fees from the school boards. It is also important to note that the boards had to guarantee attendance for all children in their respective districts between the ages of 5 and 13, and to that end, they could appoint officers to enforce attendance. As employees of State-funded structures (namely, the school boards) those engaged in enforcing school attendance – *the board men* – can appropriately claim to hold the longest pedigree amongst current social work groups. (However, children could leave school at the age of ten if a prescribed level of educational achievement had been achieved.)

The emergence of school attendance enforcement

We need to begin this section by reminding ourselves that British law, as noted by Johns (2005, p44), does not, and never has, required children to attend *school*, but only to be *educated*. Governesses and tutors often educated the children of the upper classes at home, and Parliament would never have sanctioned the legal requirement to attend *school* (remember that no member of the British Royal Family had ever attended school, prior to Prince Charles in the 1950s, so Parliament could never have enacted legislation that ran the risk of the monarch and other members of the aristocracy being prosecuted). That said, the Education Act 1880 required those children not *educated otherwise* to attend school, and hence the business of school attendance enforcement began.

Once something, such as school attendance, becomes compulsory, a new language becomes needed for those who deviate from the required norm, by not attending. It is instructive to note that a Middle Ages term for abuse in relation to a *beggar* or *rogue* – namely, a *truant* – became adopted as the accepted term for the child not attending school. (It is also significant to note that such an indiscriminate and stigmatising term has been uncritically absorbed into the government lexicon with the emergence of such strategic developments as truancy sweeps, which we will review in Chapter 5.) Having passed the law about attendance, and labelled the problematic person and deed – *truant and truancy* – the State needed to define a role to enforce attendance.

School attendance officers (or *board men*, as they were commonly known) became one of those menacing figures firmly implanted in the minds of young schoolboys and girls, a type of *folk devil* (to adapt Stan Cohen's memorable phrase). This figure was expected to be an effective deterrent in *playing truant*, and made all the more menacing because the child could only picture him in his imagination (if s/he faithfully attended school, that is).

Once instituted, compulsory elementary education rapidly removed young people from the adult arena into the specific space that defined the separation of children – the school. In England, the proportion of children aged 5–14 attending schooling rose from 24 per cent in 1870 to 48 per cent in 1880 and thence to 70 per cent by 1900.

However not everyone was willing, or able, to send their children to school. In London in 1889, there were 13,000 summonses issued against parents for the non-attendance of their children, and in England and Wales as a whole there were nearly 100,000 prosecutions for truancy in the 1880s – with the offence being second only to drunkenness in terms of court appearances.

As Cunningham suggests (1995, p159), *from the state's point of view, compulsory schooling provided opportunities for surveillance beyond anything that could be hoped for in the home*. Indeed, Davin (1996) asserts that schools as *beacons of civilisation* have always been about monitoring and control. The emergence of compulsory education, along with the universal provision of midwifery and health visiting services, from the first decade of the twentieth century, served to identify the *residuum* – those families who did not avail themselves of these *New Jerusalem* services (Hunt, 2004).

In 1902, responsibility for schools passed to *those great public assemblies* (in the words of Arthur Balfour) – the borough councils and the county councils – which indeed remains the state of affairs for most schools to the present day.

Following the debacle of such a high number of potential young recruits being rejected for service in the Boer War on medical grounds, the influential *Report of the Interdepartmental Committee on the Physical Deterioration of the Young* (1904) led to schools becoming the focus for health improvement via the Education (Provision of Meals) Act 1906, the provision of school medical inspections, and the establishment of health visitors as a means to monitor the health and welfare of all infants (Hill, 2004, p19).

According to Hunt (2004, p246) Joseph Chamberlain *championed education not out of trepidation, but from a conviction that it remained the finest mechanism both for working-class self-improvement and for broader class harmony*. Such sentiments were equally in evidence in the inter-war period, with the influential *Hadow Report* stating that: *What a wise and good parent would desire for his own children, that a nation must desire for all children* (Board of Education, 1931, pxxix). (The idea that schools should be the prime location for health improvement – as well as moral and intellectual development – has been recently resurrected with the populist campaign for the return of school meals to address Britain's modern day equivalencies to rickets – namely obesity and general lack of fitness.)

(Butler's) Education Act of 1944, comprehensives and beyond

The Education Act 1944 – one leg of the Welfare State triangular stool, along with the National Health Service and the social security system – introduced a tripartite scheme at secondary level, namely grammar (or selective) schools, secondary modern schools and technical schools. Whilst the latter are largely forgotten, it is the contentious use of selection at the age of 11 that resulted in a particular critique of the arrangements and which contributed to the breakdown of the post-war social policy consensus (known as Butskillism) in the 1960s. The development of comprehensive schools from that decade onwards was part of the government's desire to use education as a vital weapon of social engineering, to promote social justice (Hendrick, 2003) and such a policy assumed that all children and young people would be able to take equal advantage of broader and more open opportunities.

In terms of services to achieve compulsory school attendance, education welfare officers (EWOs) replaced school attendance officers in the 1940s, and alongside the local authority childcare committees, the service also provided poor families with school dinners, uniforms and education. In other words, their remit extended beyond the *control* function into what we would now see as contributing to family support services. However, the enforcement agenda was reinforced by the Children and Young Persons Act of 1969, which set out the grounds for care proceedings – whereby a child or young person could be made subject to a supervision or care order – which included not going to school or not receiving an education as a ground alongside committing an offence, being in moral danger and having impairment of health and welfare. As a consequence of such broad categories, the period after the implementation of the Children and Young Persons Act 1969 (in the early 1970s) saw the highest number of children (as a percentage) being in local authority care.

The anomalous persistence of selective education and grammar schools (and consequentially of secondary modern schools) in a small number of local authorities has provided a springboard for the fragmentation of contemporary school formations, accelerated by the proposals of the Education Bill 2006 (see Chapter 10) for the establishment of trust schools and the acceleration of separation of schools from the control of local education authorities. Nevertheless, New Labour's policies are allegedly informed by Old Labour values of *education as emancipation, an antidote to social exclusion, handmaid of social justice* (Toynbee and Walker, 2001, p44).

The rise and fall of segregated special education: Tiny steps towards school inclusion

Before we end this brief historical survey of education and social care, we need to consider the position of what is now called *special education*, and which relates to educational provision for disabled children or those defined as having special educational needs. In terms of education, it is worth noting that *under the 1944 Education Act, children with learning disabilities were described as 'ineducable' and it was not until 1971 that children with learning disabilities became entitled to education, but this was in special schools according to the diagnosis of disability* (Hughes, 2005, p85). In fact, traditionally, disabled children had received either no education at all, or had been progressively segregated into special schools, many of which were boarding schools, and which therefore served to segregate children not only educationally, but also socially.

However, the progressive notion of inclusive education gained momentum from the 1970s, with the publication of the *Warnock Report* (DES, 1978). The inquiry had said it was wrong to identify children by means of their *handicap*, and that it was preferable to see children as children first, with additional special educational needs (SEN), which should be identified and then addressed accordingly. Thus began the process of reversing centuries of segregating children with special needs from *mainstream* education.

> *Ordinary schools must expect to cater for more children with special needs and the whole concept of provision for children with peculiar difficulties, or indeed peculiar talents, must become a natural part of the comprehensive ideal.*
> (Warnock, 1980 cited in Chitty, 2004, p193)

Accordingly, the Education Act 1981 introduced the Statement of Special Educational Needs system, as a mechanism for defining the additional needs of a range of disabled children and young people, based upon the assumption that such needs would be met, wherever possible, within mainstream education.

Following the Education Act 1993, each school was required to appoint a Special Educational Needs Co-ordinator (a SENCO), who now works to implement the Special Educational Needs and Disability Act 2001 (see Chapter 3).

So we arrive at the Education Act 1996 that is couched, as noted by Calman (2001, p131), within a policy of presumed *inclusion*, whereby *the child with special educational needs should normally be educated in mainstream schools, as long as this is compatible with:*

a) his receiving the special educational provision which his learning difficulty calls for;

b) the provision of efficient education for the children with whom he will be educated; and

c) the efficient use of resources.

In terms of ideas about inclusive education and the rights of those with special needs, it is worthwhile to reflect again upon your own educational experiences, and in particular recall the extent to which your schooling embraced diversity.

ACTIVITY 1.2

How inclusive was your education? Were you educated alongside disabled children or those with identified special needs such as Sarbjit and Rebecca on page xix? If it was the case, what kinds of additional needs were appropriately met within your school?

Comment

The fact is that the progressive inclusion of children and young people with specific additional needs has gathered apace in terms of pupils with mobility issues and sensory impairments, whereas progress has been very different in relation to both intellectual difference and learning disability, and in terms of behavioural difficulties.

We will return to this question in Chapter 5, when arguments for and against inclusive education will be examined. A theme consistently addressed within this book is the extent to which the principle of school inclusion is compatible with the objective of raising standards. The idea of school inclusion might be simply acceptable to all in terms of children with physical disabilities, but to what extent is there a consensus about including children with learning disabilities?

From our experiences to our practice

Before we move away from this brief historical summary, it is instructive to acknowledge that our own perceptions of the education of others will be significantly affected by our own experiences of school. If the new agenda is to locate education at the heart of children's services, with social work and education welfare operating within the arena of full service extended schools, and within educationally driven children's centres, then the practitioner's experiences of schooling, and of teachers, will significantly impact upon her/his capacity for inter-professional learning and inter-professional practice.

ACTIVITY 1.3

What do you most clearly remember about school – at the primary and secondary levels?

Try to identify who you consider to be good or bad teachers, and why?

Comment

Anecdotal evidence would all seem to suggest some quite consistent themes about the qualities attributed to those seen as *good* teachers. These qualities revolve around consistency of approach, and are about making children feel secure by being *in charge* or *in control*, by operating fair but firm discipline regimes, by maintaining the boundary between the adult and child worlds, by not trying too hard to impress young people, and by having a passion and commitment for the job (not going through the motions).

Beyond the specifics of the *teaching* role, there would appear to be a set of ethics that can be applied across the practice range with children and young people (which are summarised by the General Teaching Council, 2002).

In Chapter 2, we will examine the key features of the Children Act 2004, which is destined to fundamentally alter the structures within which social work in children's services and education is to take place.

FURTHER READING

Chitty, C (2004) *Education policy in Britain*. Basingstoke: Palgrave.

Whitty, G (2002) *Making sense of education policy*. London: Paul Chapman.

These two texts are both really helpful summaries of the evolution of policies concerning education, schooling and the role of the State.

Chapter 2

The Children Act 2004: Requirements and the key principles

… those historically left on the margins of policy advances should now be central to the shared agenda for reducing inequalities and making 'every child matter'.
(Chase, Jackson and Simon, 2006, p4)

Education goes to the heart of all that we stand for as a party, and everything we are doing – and still need to do – to make Britain a fairer and more equal society.
(Blair, 2004, p1)

Background to the Act and the five core outcomes

We cannot over-emphasise our view that the role of teachers is of prime importance. It is he or she who, seeing the child daily in class, is often the first to become aware that all is not well. (Seebohm Report, 1968, para 216, p64).

It may seem somewhat ironic that we begin this introduction to the Children Act 2004 – which, in the wake of the death of Victoria Climbié, enacts the final demise of social services departments with the creation of children's services – with a reference back to the *Seebohm Report* of 1968, which heralded the introduction of generic practice. Nevertheless, the point of the quotation is that the Seebohm Committee recognises the centrality of universal service provision – education in schools – as the bedrock of services for all children, young people and their families.

When introducing the Children Act 2004 the then Minister for Children, Margaret Hodge, stated *the government's five-year strategy for children and learners reaffirms our commitment to high-quality childcare for all, giving children a good start in life, and supporting parents in their choices*. These seem to be laudable and incontrovertible goals, not necessarily requiring legislation. So, why did the Government introduce this far-reaching piece of legislation, which replaces social services departments with new structures?

To answer the question, we need to reflect upon the appalling circumstances surrounding the death of Victoria Climbié in 2000, which resulted in the Government setting up the Laming Inquiry, and which ultimately led to the publication of the Green Paper *Every Child Matters*, in 2003. Although many commentators expected the paper to focus upon the specifics of child protection systems (and their failure in this tragic case), the report in fact recommended far-reaching structural changes to the delivery of all services to children, young people and families.

Various reasons have been offered subsequently as to why children's services need to be transformed: that too many children do not reach their potential and remain socially excluded; that too many children are harmed and abused (e.g. Victoria Climbié); that services are reactive and fragmented; that the children's workforce itself is segmented; and that UK society remains other than child centered. To respond to these concerns, the Change for Children programme demands a radical transformation of services through new structures, a reframing of how children and families receive universal services, and an integration of targeted and specialist services.

Many assert that such change would have come about without the *Climbié Report*, and as Parton pertinently notes (2006, p151) the Green Paper was *primarily concerned with taking forward the government's proposals for reforming children's services which it had been developing for some years*. Indeed, we can see from the following quotation – predating the Climbié inquiry and the publication of *Every Child Matters* – that the Government's Children and Young People's Unit (CYPU) had already determined a *vision* for young people in terms of the need to ensure that:

Every child and young person deserves the best possible start in life, to be brought up in a safe, happy and secure environment, to be consulted, listened to and heard, to be supported as they develop into adulthood and maturity, and be given every opportunity to achieve their full potential. (CYPU, 2001, p2)

To many observers, such aspirations for all children, whilst branded into the new language of *mission speak*, represent nothing new in terms of traditional Labour Party values. What is new are the means to achieve such goals. This difference is represented by an abandonment of traditional Social Democratic cornerstone policies (such as comprehensive schools, redistributive tax policies and free higher education) and a commitment to a Third Way child, youth and family policy (Mizzen, 2003, p457).

Models of child welfare services

The creation of a paradigm comparing the interconnected perspectives of child welfare policy, as developed by Fox Harding (1997), helps us to locate the new legislation in its historical context. The introduction of the Children Act 2004 is firmly rooted in the two distinct yet interconnected policy perspectives of *State Paternalism* and *Kinship Defenders*. On the one hand, the Government seeks to empower communities and to enable families to do the best by their children, by ensuring they achieve their educational potential, developed within a culture of respectful and acceptable behaviour, and ensuring their safety from various risks. At the same time, the legislation affirms the conviction that the well-being of all children is the concern of the State, which will intervene if the welfare of any child is being impaired, and the State will accordingly award itself the power to retain ever more information of every child's development in terms of health, education and behaviour.

The Children Act of 2004, in affirming that all children come under the purview of the State, has created the following hierarchical model as a way of locating those in greatest need within the context of all children and their universal services.

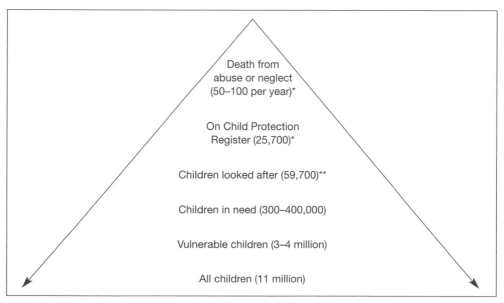

Death from
abuse or neglect
(50–100 per year)*

On Child Protection
Register (25,700)*

Children looked after (59,700)**

Children in need (300–400,000)

Vulnerable children (3–4 million)

All children (11 million)

* These children may or may not be on the Child Protection Register, or looked after, or vulnerable.
** These children are included in the children in need figure, and not all children on the Child Protection Register are looked after.

Figure 2.1 *Hierarchical model of locating children in greatest need*

Source: Every Child Matters (Chief Secretary to the Treasury, 2003, p15).

Furthermore, it has taken the unique and unprecedented step of defining specific outcomes for *all* children and young people, with the result that *all services* will be measured against the following *five core outcomes*:

- enjoying and achieving;
- staying safe;
- being healthy;
- making a positive contribution;
- economic well-being.

These five outcomes translate into 25 specific aims, which in turn form the basis of each local authority's children and young people's plan (CYPP).

How are the outcomes to be achieved?

The defined outcomes are to be achieved via the ten elements of the national framework:

(1) a duty to co-operate to promote the well-being of children and young people;

(2) a duty to make arrangements to safeguard and promote the welfare of children and young people;

(3) the development of statutory Local Safeguarding Children's Boards (LSCBs) to replace the non-statutory Area Child Protection Committees (ACPCs);

(4) the appointment of local directors of children services;

(5) the establishment of a National Service Framework for Children, Young People and Maternity Services;

(6) the outcomes framework;

(7) the development of an integrated inspection framework;

(8) the appointment of a Children's Commissioner;

(9) the development of a common assessment framework; and

(10) workforce reform to help develop skills and to ensure appropriate staffing levels.

Who will make them happen?

The issue of how various professions can best work together to meet the needs of service users lies at the heart of the concept of organisational realignment and the lead professional role (see below).

Nearly 30 years ago, Katrin Fitzherbert stated in *Child Care Services and the Teacher* (1977) that: *The different facets of a child's growth and development are so inter-dependent that they make nonsense of a division of our helping profession into separate and often antagonistic camps* (quoted in Jackson, 2001, p18). Now, in the first decade of the twenty-first century, the Children Act of 2004 attempts to address those very concerns, by placing a new duty on agencies to co-operate to improve the well-being of children and young people (see element 1 above). This duty, which provides the basis for the children's trust approach, provides for integrated planning and commissioning of services through local partnerships. In essence, the Act reflects the Government's long-term vision to integrate services for children within a single organisational focus. Therefore, the legislation requires every top-tier or unitary local authority in England to appoint a Director of Children's Services (under section 18) and to designate a Lead Member for Children's Services (under section 19). The Act allows authorities complete flexibility over the organisational arrangements below these two posts, and all local authorities are required to have such arrangements in place by 2008.

Which agencies are to be involved?

(Section 11, Children Act 2004)
Children's services authorities (those authorities that currently provide social services and which are education authorities) may develop partnerships with other organisations, such as police authorities, Probation Boards, strategic health authorities, NHS Trusts and Foundation Trusts, Primary Care Trusts (PCTs), Youth Offending Teams, local prisons or secure training centres, the Learning and Skills Councils and district councils (where relevant). This statutory duty to co-operate commenced on 1 April 2005.

Local Safeguarding Children Boards (LSCBs)

(Sections 13–16 (England) and sections 31–34 (Wales) Children Act 2004)
These Boards replace Area Child Protection Committees as from April 2006, with statutory representative membership from *Board Partners* (see above), together with members from the Children and Family Court Advisory Service (CAFCASS). The Boards were required to be in place by the end of April 2006. There is a duty of co-operation between the children's services authority and the Board partners, and the purpose of LCSBs is to co-ordinate the work of Board partners for the purpose of safeguarding and promoting the welfare of children and to ensure effectiveness. Two or more children's services authorities *may* decide to form a joint LSCB, thereby co-ordinating safeguarding practices across a larger area.

Section 14 of the Children Act 2004 defines the objectives of the LSCB to:

- co-ordinate what is done by each person or body represented on the Board for the purpose of safeguarding and promoting the welfare of children in the area of the authority by which it is established; and

- ensure the effectiveness of what is done by each such person or body for these purposes.

Children and young people's plans (CYPPs)

(Section 17, Children Act 2004)
Again, from April 2006, each children's services authority is required by regulations to prepare and publish a CYPP setting out the authority's strategy for discharging functions in

relation to children and young people. The consequence of the plan is to develop a local workforce strategy, to ascertain how many workers are needed, at different qualification levels and grades, over a projected time period.

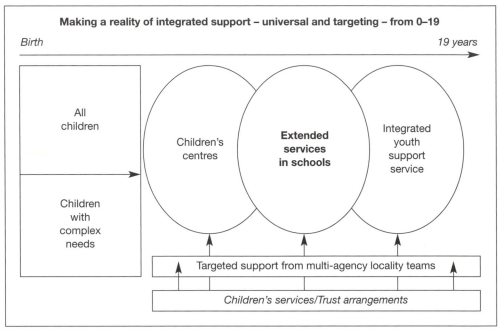

Figure 2.2 *The vision for the future*

Based upon the principle of integration, there will no longer be a requirement to produce separate education development plans, Early Years development and childcare plans, school organisation plans, behaviour support plans, class size plans, children's services plans or local authority adoption services plans. In fact, the CYPPs replace 19 existing statutory plans, so coherence and integration should be the result.

CYPPs form one of the three *partnership blocks* supported by local area agreements – safer and stronger communities, healthier communities and older people, and children and young people.

According to Bob Hudson (2005, p37), councils and local partners should follow the following guidelines when drawing up a CYPP:

- *Compare local outcomes for children and young people with the national picture.*

- *Look at outcomes for particular groups of young people, such as those with disabilities or from ethnic minorities.*

- *Use this data and draw on the views of children, young people and their families, local communities and front-line staff to analyse needs.*

- *Agree the nature and scale of the challenge, identify the resources available and set priorities for action.*

- *Plan the pattern of service most likely to secure priority outcomes, considering how fast resources can be shifted into prevention and early intervention.*

- *Decide together how best to purchase or provide services from statutory, voluntary or private providers.*

- *Plan workforce development and other changes in local processes and ways of working necessary to support delivery.*

- *Monitor and review services to ensure they are working to deliver the ambitions set out for them.*

The Children's Commissioner (England)

(Sections 1–9, Schedule I, Children Act 2004)

The Commissioner for England is responsible for promoting awareness of the views and interests of children having regard to the United Nations Convention on the Rights of the Child. The Commissioner has powers to investigate individual cases where there is a wider relevance, and will report to Parliament through the Secretary of State. The current post-holder, Professor Al Aynsley-Green, was appointed in March 2005.

A common assessment framework (CAF)

The Children Act 2004 requires local authorities to develop integrated delivery systems, using a CAF for workers in health, education, social work and other agencies. The CAF is designed to enable better-targeted referrals to other specialist services when needed so they can respond more effectively. This is to be implemented between April 2006 and the end of 2008, and will rely heavily upon the emerging role of the lead professional.

'Children with additional needs' and the lead professional role

The use of the CAF may result in a worker identifying additional needs in relation to a particular child. This is a broad term that refers to those children and young people whose experiences and characteristics may affect their capacity to thrive and who require additional support in order to achieve their potential. According to Government policy and strategic thinking, the needs of the majority of these children will be able to be met through interventions of various practitioners within the context of universal services.

However, for some children and young people, there will be a need for a co-ordinated input from two or more services. In such a situation, an integrated package of support, using targeted services, will be co-ordinated by the *lead professional*.

In particular when children or young people have multiple additional needs, then the lead professional role will *ensure professional involvement is rationalised, co-ordinated and communicated effectively*, using specialist or statutory services.

Examples of children and young people with significant or complex needs are:

- children in need;
- children looked after;
- children on the Child Protection Register;
- disabled children;
- children with statements of special educational needs;
- children and young people involved with Youth Offending Teams.

Significantly, the lead professional role may be ascribed to any of the following:

personal advisers; health visitors; midwives; youth workers; family workers; substance misuse workers; nursery nurses; education welfare officers; community children's nurses; school nurses; learning mentors.

Such anticipated flexibility mirrors and matches workforce developments in relation to adult services, where the concepts of skill mixing and inter-professional education are being heralded as the way forward to meet the targets of reducing waiting lists, and of efficiency gains that arise from breaking down traditional practice boundaries and role demarcations.

A shared database

(Section 12 (England) and section 24 (Wales), Children Act 2004)
Local authorities are to lead integrated services in the development of a shared database on children, containing information relevant to their welfare, as outlined by Secretary of State Regulations. In a letter sent to all children's service directors, the Children's Minister Beverley Hughes stated: *Our aim is to ensure that children's services in all areas have access by the end 2008 to an operational index containing basic details for all children aged zero to 18 in their area and contact details for the services they are receiving.* Significantly, the index will not contain any case records, nor anything to indicate that the child is on a Child Protection Register, nor any clinical observations, statements of school attendance or academic performance.

The database will contain the following, in relation to every one of Britain's 11.7 million children:

- a unique identifying number;

- the child's name;

- the child's age;

- the child's gender;

- basic information about the child's parent or carer;

- contact details of services associated with the child;

- a facility for practitioners to indicate that they have additional information to share, that they are taking action, or have undertaken an assessment in relation to that child.

Only authorised practitioners who have had the relevant police checks and training will be allowed access to the index.

Duty to promote the educational achievement of looked after children

The duties of authorities as corporate parents have been extended. Section 52 of the Children Act 2004 amends section 22(3)(a) of the Children Act 1989, and places a duty on the local authority to safeguard and promote the welfare of children looked after by them and includes, in particular, a duty to promote the child's educational achievement. This will be explored in more detail in Chapter 7.

The framework for inspection (Joint Area Reviews)
(Sections 20–24 Children Act 2004)

Joint Area Reviews will take place to evaluate the extent to which children's services improve the well-being of children in the area, by inspecting universal, preventative and specialist services. The new regime brings together ten inspectorates, under the leadership of the Office for Standards in Education (Ofsted), to produce a single report for each council or authority. As Mike Lee (Head of Special Projects in West Sussex) suggested: *You have to stop looking at the inputs you make and start looking at the outcomes impact on children's lives* (*Children Now*, 16–22 November 2005). Services will be inspected and evaluated against the five outcomes of *Every Child Matters* and the related judgement areas.

Children's centres

Building upon the presumed success of the targeted Sure Start programme, the concept of children's centres became a central plank of the Government's strategic plan to implement the Children Act 2004 and 3,500 children's centres are due to be in place by 2010, with many of them located on school sites.

By March 2006, children's centres are expected to have reached at least 650,000 pre-school children in the 20 per cent most disadvantaged areas across the country; by 2008 there should be 2,500 centres and by 2010, 3,500 centres – or one in every *community*.

The main role of a children's centre is to ensure services are delivered and that targets – on such things as children's health and development, access to services, and parental involvement – are all met by communicating with the community and liaising with different professionals. The centres will be directly linked into achieving the Choosing Health objectives, including reducing smoking in pregnancy, increasing breastfeeding rates, improving diet and nutrition, reducing levels of child obesity, and reducing teenage pregnancies. Different remits have been developed for centres in the 30 per cent most disadvantaged areas and for the 70 per cent more advantaged areas, and for those meeting the needs of rural communities. The universal children's centre model is designed to be integrated and consistent with the extended role for schools.

Extended schools and 'wraparound' childcare

The 9 a.m. to 3.30 p.m. deal is a thing of the past in terms of education. Of course, it's still our core purpose, but particularly with our children and parents, the time has come to look at education as far wider than just what happens in the classroom. This statement from a primary school headteacher in Islington illustrates the enthusiastic drive in some quarters for a re-examination of the historically and socially constructed notion of the school. The Government has pledged £680m to support the development of extended schools and the Department for Education and Skills (DfES) expects that every child will be able to access extended school services by 2010. In essence, all schools are required to provide access to childcare from 8 a.m. to 6 p.m. Originally mooted by the Social Exclusion Unit in 1999 in a report entitled *Schools Plus*, the purpose of the strategy is to address three linked and interconnected issues: using schools as the focus of neighbourhood regeneration; tackling educational failure by offering a broader range of services on the same site; and using resources in a cost-effective way, given that most traditional schools are only open for about 52 per cent of the days in as year (once weekends, bank holidays and school holidays are factored in) and for only 6.5 hours out of a possible 15 (based on a 7 a.m. to 10 p.m. schedule) or the minimum ten hours expected as extended schools (by being open from 8 a.m. to 6 p.m.).

For New Labour policy leaders, there are numerous advantages.

- Schools can become more firmly established as the centres for community development, regeneration and cohesion.

- Schools are expensive resources – in terms of construction, maintenance, security, servicing – so it makes sense for facilities to be used 'round the clock'.

- Engaging parents and carers in a range of school-based activities will enhance pupil performance.

The National Foundation for Educational Research, which has described this whole project as a *quiet revolution*, has conducted a study into extended schools (see www.nfer.ac.uk

/research-areas/pims-data/outlines/schools-as-community-based-organisations-project.cfm), linked to the work of the National Remodelling Team, which has drawn upon two organisations (ContinYou and 4Children) (see www.remodelling.org/programmes/es.php). Furthermore, five councils in the Midlands – Coventry, Walsall, Dudley, Staffordshire and Worcestershire – have established a network with the charity ContinYou to improve links between extended schools and children's centres.

For primary schools, the full service extended school concept could mean:

- a swift referral system for pupils needing additional, specialist support;
- the provision of before and after-school childcare;
- after-school clubs;
- family learning classes.

Similarly, for secondary schools, the full service extended school concept could mean:

- a range of holiday activities for pupils;
- sports, arts and information technology activities for the wider community throughout the year;
- a range of other services, such as breakfast clubs, after-school clubs, facilities for community activities.

According to Pat Petrie (of the Thomas Coram Research Unit) we should be thinking about extended schools as children's spaces – as a milieu for re-evaluating the dynamic relationships between children, teachers, parents and communities whereas Helen Wheatley (2005) sees extended schools as a perfect opportunity to address the structural disadvantages confronting families of disabled children. She notes that 55 per cent of families with a disabled child are living in or on the margins of poverty, and the absence of good quality, reliable and accessible childcare is one of the biggest impediments to being able to earn more money. The facility for a disabled child to stay in school longer than at present will enhance parental choice, expand the potential for financial stability, and allow the child to be cared for in a familiar and reliable environment.

In short, it is anticipated that schools will be the epicentre for support systems for *all* children, and in particular for those in need.

However, the *big project* has its critics. Bob Holman (2004, p20) thinks the project is really all about childcare: *(T)he main purpose is the New Labour one of getting both parents or lone parents to work. In short, the economy is more important than family life*. This critique acknowledges that centralisation of services in fact undermines community life and paradoxically creates a culture of professionalisation that destroys the best efforts of mutualism and communitarian responsibility.

The Big Vision?

The former Children's Minister, Margaret Hodge, set out the Big Vision: *Integrated teams of professionals working in and around children's centres and schools will bring services more directly to families. They will be able to intervene and provide support before families reach crisis point. We want all children to have safe and secure childhoods in which they can develop their full potential. We want to see fewer children suffering from educational failure, experiencing substance misuse, committing crime and anti-social behaviour, or becoming teenage parents. That means giving greater support to vulnerable children and those in care and raising education standards for all pupils.* These are laudable sentiments, and the notion of locating targeted and specialist services within the framework of universal provision (see Figure 2.3 below) has long been an aspiration of the social work community, not least as an attempt to reduce the stigma and shame so long associated with the recipients of old-style welfare provision.

As a result, services are to be stratified in terms of being universal, targeted or specialist.

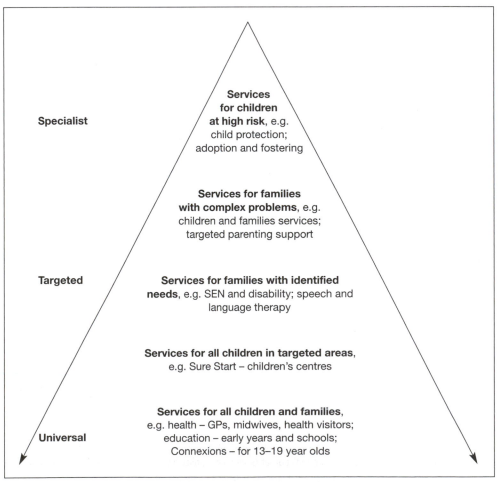

Figure 2.3 *Targeted services within a universal context*

Source: *Every Child Matters* (Chief Secretary to the Treasury, 2003, p21).

However, are the current agendas for education, social work and health compatible? The model below (Figure 2.4) indicates that the assumption is that the more specialist and complex the services, the more integrated the delivery systems. Current examples of such practice would include Child and Adolescent Mental Health Services (CAMHS) or the Youth Offending Teams (YOTs), under the auspices of the Youth Justice Board. Here we find, in the first example, social workers, child psychologists, child psychiatrists, educational psychologists, nurses, teachers and play therapists working together to provide a *seamless service*, but bringing specialist skills, knowledge, values, powers, duties and responsibilities and knowledge to the joint endeavour.

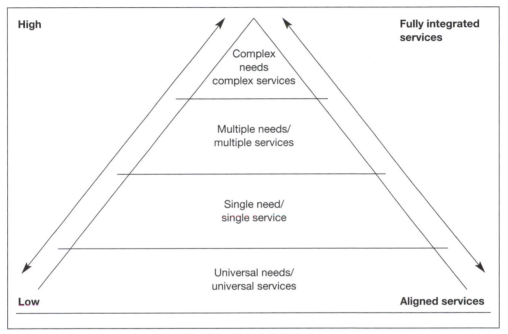

Figure 2.4 *A model for the continuum of integration*

Whilst emphasising aligned and compatible services, the Government's vision assumes that universal services – such as child health, primary and secondary education – will remain essentially single service entities, but with far higher degrees of collaboration than is currently the case.

C H A P T E R   S U M M A R Y

The Children Act 2004 presents a massive challenge to the traditional ways in which social work and associated support services have been offered to children, young people, families and communities. Similarly, the Education Bill of 2006 will also have a profound and far-reaching impact upon the schooling landscape. According to commentators such as Melissa Benn there is a glaring contradiction at Government policy level between the drive towards building strong inclusive communities and the politics of choice as evidenced by current educational reform. As she suggests, *if one school can cream off better performers then a neighbouring school will have more children with problems* (Benn, 2005, p22), and the Association of Professionals in Education and Children's Trusts warns that: *Trust schools will be free to pursue their own interests, even when this might run counter to the welfare of local children* (cited in *Children Now*, 8–14 March 2006).

These contradictions and concerns will be played out in the coming years, within the context of other elements of legislation. In the next chapter, we will look at the range of legislation within which children's services practitioners operate, beyond the Children Act 1989 and the Children Act 2004.

FURTHER READING

DfES (2003) *Every Child Matters* (Green Paper). London: The Stationery Office.

DfES (2004) *Every Child Matters: Next steps*. London: The Stationery Office.

DfES (2004) *Children Act 2004*. London: The Stationery Office.

DfES (2004) *Every Child Matters: Change for children*. London: The Stationery Office.

All of the above documents chart the progression of thinking about work with children and young people and families – from fragmented social services, education, health and allied agencies towards the goal of integrated practice within the children's services framework.

Quinney, A (2006) *Collaborative social work practice*. Exeter: Learning Matters.

This series companion text helps the practitioner/student reflect upon the tensions and dynamics of multi-disciplinary practice in relation to health, housing, youth work, justice, and education.

Chapter 3
The broader legal context of contemporary practice

Education makes a people easy to lead, but difficult to drive; easy to govern but impossible to enslave.
(Attributed to Lord Brougham (1778–1868))

… we have been innovating for student improvement for most of this century yet the extent to which this has resulted in improvement in the life chances of students is debatable.
(Michael Fullan, 1999, p1)

A C H I E V I N G   A   S O C I A L   W O R K   D E G R E E

This chapter will help you meet the following National Occupational Standards:
Key Role 5: Manage and be accountable, with supervision and support, for your own social work practice within your organisation:
- Work within multi-disciplinary and multi-organisational teams, networks and systems.
- Work within multi-disciplinary and multi-organisational teams, networks and systems.

It will also introduce you to the following academic standards as set out in the social work subject benchmark statement:
3.1.2 The service delivery context
- The issues and trends in modern public and social policy and their relationship to contemporary practice and service delivery in social work.
- The significance of legislative and legal frameworks and service delivery standards (including the nature of legal authority, the application of legislation in practice, statutory accountability and tensions between statute, policy and practice).

Introduction

In this chapter, we will review the major pieces of legislation that, alongside the Children Act 2004, make up the landscape within which educational and children's services now operate in terms of the education of vulnerable children and young people. It is not possible, in our view, for students or practitioners to be continually keeping abreast of an ever-changing legal framework. After all, the planned integrated children's services system, as outlined in Chapter 2, could result in the beleaguered practitioner feeling that they needed to understand the whole legal system concerning the specific obligations, powers and duties in relation to child health, mental health, childcare, child protection, children looked after, education, special education, education welfare, youth justice and criminal justice. This is clearly unrealistic. However, the purpose of this chapter is to enable the practitioner to gain an introductory understanding of the broader context of practice at the social work and education interface. Such an overview might enable the stressed student or hard-pressed practitioner to pursue more detailed enquiry at a later date, and as the need arises.

The law and school attendance

As implied above, it is not the purpose of this book to explore and explain the core legal framework for social work practice with children, young people and families (namely the Children Act 1989, the Child Protection Act 1999, the Children (Leaving Care) Act 2000 and the Children and Adoption Act 2002). This legislative context is explored elsewhere in the *Transforming Social Work Practice* series (see Jowitt and O'Loughlin, 2005 and Johns, 2005).

However, a cornerstone of this text is about the importance of education in determining and shaping the life opportunities of children, young people and adults. It is therefore appropriate to begin this section with an explanation and exploration of the legislation that deems *education* to be a compulsory aspect of the childhood experience within Britain, as outlined historically in Chapter 2.

Since 1880, the law in England and Wales has stated that children must be educated between specific age ranges. Elementary education was first made compulsory for children aged from 5 to 10, rising thereafter to 11 (1893), to 14 (1918), to 15 (1944) and thence, from 1972, to the current minimum school leaving age of 16. Interestingly enough, the lower-age limit of five has remained consistent throughout this period – it is the upper-age limit that has been progressively extended over the past 120 years. Before we proceed with exploring the legislation, it is instructive to reflect upon the arbitrary nature of these childhood milestones.

Why from 5 to 16?

ACTIVITY 3.1

We know that children begin schooling later in other northern European countries, and we also know that the majority of children are attending school from when aged four in the UK, or even earlier. As we have seen in Chapter 2, government policy – linking the provision of quality daycare in children's centres and extended schooling to parental capacity for working and economic independence (from benefits) – would all point to reducing the age of beginning compulsory education to four, or even lower.

*At what age do you think children should be **required** to be educated, and is there a case for extending the school leaving age to above 16?*

Comment

There is, of course, no right or wrong answer, other than to recognise the socially constructed nature of such legal requirements for education. The fact remains that the State has, for over 120 years, chosen to enforce the education of children from the age of five onwards, up to varying ages.

The core parental duty regarding education

Parents (by which we mean those with parental responsibility, as defined by the Children Act 1989) have a legal duty to ensure that their children receive an education either by attendance at school or *otherwise*. The responsibility of parents/guardians is clearly established in section 7 of the Education Act 1996:

> *The parent of every child of compulsory school age shall cause them to receive efficient full-time education suitable:*
>
> *(a) to his/her age ability and aptitude, and*
>
> *(b) to any special education needs he may have, either by regular attendance at school or otherwise.*

It is important to recognise that parents can fulfil their duty by *either* ensuring their child attends school *or* equally by making alternative arrangements to educate the child themselves. If parents elect to educate their child themselves they are responsible for providing all the necessary materials and resources. Parents can, at any time, re-admit their child to a school. (See Chapter 6 for an exploration of home education.) Furthermore, there are various organisations that offer support and advice to parents who elect to educate their children at home (see Appendix 3). However, if the local education authority (LEA) is not satisfied that the child is receiving a suitable education it must serve a notice on the parents requiring them to provide proof of the child's education (see the School Attendance Orders section).

The legal duties placed on parents are long-standing, but the increased focus of Government attention on holding parents to account in terms of their exercising of this duty has a more recent history. Since the 1990s the Government has, through its Social Exclusion Unit, produced evidence to identify the links between disaffection and impaired life chances and has made absence and poor behaviour a national priority (as illustrated in the Introduction). However, the effectiveness of the Government's drive to raise attendance and to tackle truancy has been disputed, as discussed in Chapter 9. Nevertheless, the legal options introduced to address school absence require fuller understanding. The Government has reinforced the legislation surrounding the requirement for full-time education through the institution of a higher-level offence (section 444(1A) of the Education Act 1996), which can result in imprisonment. Furthermore, the Government has sought to increase parental accountability through the establishment of measures within the Antisocial Behaviour Act 2003. By publishing frequent statistical surveys of LEA returns, the Government monitors the use of the available legal sanctions, and through the issue of guidance and good practice guidance, encourages their use.

The grounds of an offence

An offence has been committed only where a child's absence is *unauthorised* by the school, (i.e. no valid reason has been given or permission for absence has not been sought). Indeed, where absence is *authorised*, the school has *de facto*, accepted that the reasons given are valid. The are in fact two types of offences in relation to school absence.

The main offence
If a child of compulsory school age who is a registered pupil at a school fails to attend regularly at the school, his parent is guilty of an offence (Education Act 1996 (section 444)).

The aggravated offence
Since March 2001 there has been a more serious offence requiring proof that the parents or carer knew that their child was absent from school without reasonable cause: *If a parent knows that his child is failing to attend regularly at the school and fails without reasonable justification to cause him to do so* (Education Act 1996 (section 444(IA), as amended by the Criminal Justice and Court Services Act 2000). (The Education Act of 2005 extends this to include pupils who are attending alternative provision (section 116/section 444ZA, appendage to section 444 of the Education Act 1996)).

The State's response

Matters of judgement have to be made in terms of the State's response, as clearly parents are not prosecuted for every absence in relation to their child or children. There are considerations of frequency, of intent, of impact. It is important to note that, in the first instance, the Government has sought to improve overall attendance rates by targeting particular forms of absence. By addressing the range and duration of some forms of authorised absence – such as those resulting from holidays, family visits, bereavements and for religious observation – it can be said that effort is being directed at *easier and softer* targets than absence due to school disaffection and disengagement. Nevertheless, even with this approach, there are the inherent and intrinsic risks of allegations of cultural insensitivity, antagonism and charges of discrimination and unreasonableness on the part of the school. Many children from Asian communities have periods of extended absence from school in order to visit relatives in the countries of their ethnic origin, or as the consequence of family loss and bereavement. For schools to take a *tough* line on such absences runs the risk of alienating communities who are highly supportive of education, and for whom school attendance and achievement are prized and valued cultural norms.

> ## Legal Case Note (March 2006)
> *The High Court has ruled that schools – not parents or magistrates – must decide whether pupils can be taken out of school for holidays during term time. Bromley LEA had prosecuted a mother for taking her three daughters on two unauthorised holidays. Magistrates acquitted her, and the LEA appealed. The judges found in favour of the LEA, stating that the magistrates had been misdirected in acquitting the mother of the charge of being in breach of the Education Act 1996, for failing to secure the attendance of her children at their primary school. The judges ruled that* leave of absence *meant leave granted by the school.*

So, how does the State actually intervene if a child does not appear to be being educated consistently?

Intervention options

The defined professional body, the education welfare service, can chose to do a number of things by way of a response to a breach of this legislation. There are various options available, which are set out below in an ascending tariff of seriousness.

Level 1: Case work – advice, guidance and support

It would be highly misleading to imply that the education welfare service begins to intervene from the perspective of legal enforcement. In fact, education welfare practice with children, young people and their parents, carers and schools essentially uses a range of social work principles, values, skills and techniques in common with children's services social work. To illustrate the point, we will explore the practitioner's toolkit in Chapter 8. However, in this chapter we need to examine the legal options available in terms of school enforcement.

Level 2: Parenting contracts

If a pupil fails to attend school regularly, the LEA or governing body of the school may consider whether it would be appropriate to offer a parenting contract to the parent. A parenting contract is a formal written agreement between a parent and either the LEA or the governing body of a school and should contain:

- a statement by the parent that they agree to comply for a specified period with whatever requirements are specified in the contract; and

- a statement by the LEA or governing body agreeing to provide support to the parent for the purpose of complying with the contract.

Entry into a parenting contract is voluntary. The parent cannot be compelled to enter into a parenting contract if they do not wish to do so. Equally, there is no obligation on the LEA or governing body to offer a parenting contract in cases of non-attendance. Parenting contracts will, however, often be a useful tool in identifying and focusing on the issues behind the non-attendance and in developing a productive relationship with parents to address these issues.

Failure to comply with the parenting contract cannot lead to action for breach of contract or for civil damages. There is no direct sanction for a parent's failure to comply with or refusal to sign a parenting contract. However, if the pupil's irregular attendance continues or escalates to such a level where a prosecution is deemed appropriate, this should be presented as evidence in the case.

Parenting contracts can apply to parents of pupils of any type of school.

Assessing the appropriateness of a parenting contract

In deciding whether a parenting contract might be appropriate, the LEA or governing body should consider all the issues behind the non-attendance, in particular whether attendance may be improved through working with the parent and providing support to them and, if so, what form this support should take.

Level 3: School attendance orders

If it appears to a local education authority that a child of compulsory school age in their area is not receiving suitable education, either by regular attendance at school or otherwise, they shall serve a notice in writing on the parent requiring him to satisfy them within the period specified in the notice that the child is receiving such education (Education Act 1996 (section 437)).

Failure to comply with a school attendance order

If a parent on whom a school attendance order is served fails to comply with the requirements of the order, he is guilty of an offence, unless he proves that he is causing the child to receive suitable education otherwise than at school (Education Act 1996 (section 443)).

So, an offence has been committed by virtue of there being no improvement following the school attendance order. What can the LEA do next?

Level 4 option A: Penalty notices

Penalty notices for truancy were introduced in 2004, via subsection (1) of section 23 of the Anti-social Behaviour Act of 2003, which adds two new sections (444A and 444B) after section 444 of the Education Act 1996. The penalty notices are intended to be an alternative to prosecution under section 444(1) of the Education Act 1996. The notices enable parents to discharge potential liability for conviction for that offence by paying a penalty. The offence of irregular attendance has not changed. The local authority is required to issue a code of conduct setting out how the penalty notice scheme will operate in their area. The idea is that they are quicker and cheaper alternatives to prosecution for parents who fail to ensure their child's regular attendance at school, and represent a less legalistic mode of intervention.

What are they?

It is important to recognise that education welfare officers, headteachers or police officers can issue such notices. Recipients must pay £50 within 28 days, or £100 within 42 days, or face prosecution. Parents who have been fined cannot be prosecuted for the offence whilst the payment timescale is operative. However, if the parent fails to pay, then the LEA must either take the parent to court for the offence of failing to ensure regular attendance, or withdraw the notice. Penalties are to be paid to the LEA. If there is a prosecution it will follow the usual procedures of a prosecution for irregular attendance. Prosecutions will be brought by the LEA under section 444 of the Education Act 1996 (see the next section below).

How often have they been used?

Between September 2004 and September 2005, 2,700 penalty notices were issued in England.

Level 4 option B: Prosecution

There are two offences for non-attendance under the Education Act 1996 – section 444(1) and (1A).

Under section 444(1), the LEA need only show that the child failed to attend regularly at the school without authorisation. The only evidence that the LEA needs to produce to the court in this instance is the certificate of attendance. It is not necessary to obtain evidence through interview with the parent or to use such evidence at court. The LEA need not, therefore, follow the Codes of Practice when prosecuting under section 444(1). Nor, for the same reason, need LEAs follow the codes in issuing a fixed penalty notice. However, as a matter of good practice, LEAs should act in accordance with the spirit of the codes in carrying out any interviews, in particular in relation to ensuring that the parent's needs are taken into account.

Under section 444(1A), the LEA must show not only that the child failed to attend regularly at school without authorisation, but that the parent knew and failed without reasonable justification to cause the child to do so. If prosecuting under this section, the LEA may well conduct interviews with the parent to ascertain the extent of their knowledge of the non-attendance and whether they have a reasonable justification. Failure to follow the PACE codes (see below) in any such interview may seriously jeopardise a prosecution if the interview produces evidence on which the LEA wishes to rely.

Police and Criminal Evidence Act (PACE)

The Police and Criminal Evidence Act 1984 (PACE) which came into effect in 1986 sets out the conduct of investigating officers and those charging and cautioning offenders should observe. LEAs are required to have full regard for the PACE requirements when conducting casework and legal proceedings in respect of non-school attendance.

Before prosecuting a parent the LEA must consider whether to apply for an education supervision order instead of, or as well as, prosecuting.

Legal proceedings

Evidence to be presented to court

The key piece of evidence is a certificate of attendance provided by the child's school and signed by the headteacher. Other evidence may include:

- medical certificates;

- copies of warning letters;

- records of meetings;

- documentary evidence relating to aggravating circumstances;

- a report from the school.

Defences

The child shall not be deemed to have failed to attend school regularly if the parent can prove one or more of the following:

- the pupil's absence was authorised by the school; or

- the pupil was ill or prevented from attending by any unavoidable cause; or

- the absence was on a day exclusively set aside for religious observance by the religious body to which the parent belongs; or

- the school is not within walking distance of the child's home and the LEA has made no arrangements for:

  - the child's transport to and from school; or

  - boarding accommodation at or near the school; or

  - enabling the child to attend a school nearer their home; or

- the parent can show that their trade or business requires them to travel, and the child attended as regularly as the nature of the trade or business allows, and the child has attended school for at least 200 sessions during the preceding 12 months.

Court disposal options

Following a conviction the court may choose from a range of disposals:

- adjournment;

- absolute discharge;

- conditional discharge;

- fine;

- deferred sentence;

- community sentence;

- custodial sentence (only available under section 444(1A)).

Education supervision orders

Before instituting proceedings for an offence under section 443 or 444 [of the Education Act 1996] a local education authority shall consider whether it would be appropriate (instead of or as well as instituting the proceedings) to apply for an education supervision order with respect to the child (Education Act 1996 (section 447)).

This provision falls within the Children Act 1989, which states that the supervisor is under a duty to advise, *assist and befriend and give directions to* (section 35(1)(a)) *the child and the child's parents/carers in such a way as will secure that the child is properly educated.*

Before applying for an education supervision order (ESO) the following must be considered.

- The level of co-operation from parental/carer.
- The outcome of consultation with social services (an ESO cannot be made in respect of a child that is already the subject of a care order, or in the care of the local authority). (The LEA has a duty to consult with the local authority.)
- Reasonable efforts have been made to solve school attendance problems without resort to legal sanctions.
- The *no order* principle is considered, i.e. will having the order have greater benefit for the child than not having an order.

The Family Court is less formal than the magistrates' court. Attendees are positioned around a table and it is unlikely that there will be a witness box or magistrate's bench.

Possible outcomes

There are only three possible outcomes to an application for an ESO.

(1) The court does not grant the order.

(2) The court does grant the order.

(3) The court requests further investigation of the child's circumstances (this will be carried out by the children's dervices department).

ESOs should ensure that the child will receive an appropriate education and are normally granted for 12 months or until the child ceases to be of compulsory school age if that period is less than 12 months. The order will take the form of a programme of work by all involved parties and the order may include directions for the parents and the child. If parents fail to comply with a direction, they may be guilty of an offence unless they can prove that the direction was unreasonable or that they made every effort to comply.

The role of the supervising officer is to *advise assist and befriend* the young person and to have responsibility for the management and discharge of the order.

Where the child persistently fails to comply with the order, the supervisor must refer the matter to the social services department who have a duty to investigate and to commence care proceedings if necessary.

Parenting orders

Parenting orders were introduced within the provisions of section 16 of the Crime and Disorder Act 1998 and may be used as a disposal for offences under section 443 or 444 of the Education Act 1996. The magistrates must be satisfied that the order would be beneficial in preventing the commission of further offences under those sections. The order cannot be a sentence in its own right and is, therefore, an additional measure to any other disposal used. Before making an order, the court is required to consider the circumstances of the child and family and the likely impact of any order. This information may be provided verbally or by the submission of a report. Parenting orders are designed to support parents in addressing their child's difficulties rather than being a punishment. The order may be made against both parents and their consent is not required.

Orders are usually granted for a period of one year. The order comprises two elements.

(1) The parent is required to attend parenting support classes or guidance sessions which will offer help in dealing with the behaviour of their child. This is the main element of the order and may last for up to three months. The sessions may be organised in various ways and may be group or one-to-one sessions. The organisation sessions should not interfere with a parent's work or religious practices. The number of sessions should be between 6–12, with no more than one per week.

(2) The order may also include a requirement for parents to comply with specific directions which may include ensuring that their child attends school regularly or that their child is home by a specified time.

The order is overseen by a responsible officer whose role is to ensure that the parenting support sessions are arranged and that the parents comply with any requirements. Failure of a parent to comply with an order will require the supervising officer to seek to re-engage the parents and, if this is unsuccessful, to consider breach proceedings which may result in a prosecution for the breach of the order.

ACTIVITY 3.2

In the light of the above legal intervention options, consider the following case study, and suggest an action plan.

CASE STUDY

Danielle is in Year 10. Since the beginning of the academic year her school attendance has deteriorated to less than 25 per cent from its previously satisfactory level. Now six months into her GCSE course, she is significantly behind with her work, homework is rarely submitted and attempts by the school to support Danielle have failed. She has now refused to attend at all, saying that school does her head in and that the staff members routinely pick on her. Her case is the subject of a discussion between the schoolteachers and the education welfare service. Despite attempts to involve them, Danielle's family does not appear concerned about her absence.

You are working for the education welfare service. What would be your recommendation?

Comment

The lack of parental involvement and concern would make this a difficult case to work with. The absence of parental co-operation would appear to rule out advice, guidance and support with the family, or the option of an ESO. However, the first option would be to try to understand why Danielle has suddenly dipped in her attendance, and so working with the school and Danielle would be the best option. (See Chapter 4 for ways to understand school absences.)

Special educational needs and disability

Education Act 1996 and children with special educational needs

Under the Education Act 1996 (section 312), a child is defined as having special educational needs if he or she has a learning difficulty, which calls for special educational provision to be made. A learning difficulty is defined as the child: (a) having a significantly greater difficulty in learning than the majority of children his age; and (b) having a disability which prevents or hinders the child from making use of educational facilities of a kind generally provided for children of his age in schools within the area of the local authority.

Under this Act the statementing process will be undertaken, to determine whether the local education authority should issue a Statement of Special Educational Needs (*the Statement*). This is *a formal document recording the child's special educational needs and then setting out the special educational provision required to meet those needs* (Calman 2001, p130). Section 316 (as amended by the Special Educational Needs and Disability Act 2001) places a duty on local education authorities to educate children with special educational needs in mainstream schools. Section 319 of the Act also enables the local authority in certain circumstances, to provide education otherwise than in a school for children with special educational needs.

The Disability Discrimination Act 1995 and Special Educational Needs and Disability Act 2001 (SENDA)

The Disability Discrimination Act 1995, as amended by the Special Educational Needs and Disability Act 2001 (SENDA) places a duty on all schools and LEAs to increase over time the accessibility of schools for disabled pupils and to implement their plans. The 2001 Act, implemented from 1 September 2002, outlines the legal rights for disabled students in pre and post-16 education. In essence, the Act deems it unlawful for responsible bodies to treat a disabled person *less favourably* than a non-disabled person for a reason that relates to the person's disability. Children with special educational needs have a right to a place in mainstream school, and such schools can only refuse to accept them if they can prove that the education of other children will suffer.

If a disabled person is at a *substantial disadvantage* then responsible bodies are required to take 'reasonable steps' to prevent that disadvantage. Such steps might include:

- changes to policies and practices;

- changes to course requirements or work placements;

- change to the physical features of a building;

- the provision of interpreters or other support workers;

- the delivery of courses in alternative ways; and

- the provision of materials in other formats.

In essence, the Act provides stronger rights for children with specific, special or additional needs to be educated in mainstream schools, and gives specific duties to LEAs to provide advice and information for parents. As to how this is interpreted varies from one local authority to another (as we will see in Chapter 6).

Carers and Disabled Children Act 2000

The legislation essentially extended the rights of carers' recognition and assessment to young carers and extended the potential for direct payments for young disabled people – thereby bringing services for young disabled people in line with services for supporting vulnerable adults.

Education and Inspections Bill 2006

It is not the purpose of this book to examine the broad policy directions of this Bill – which has been so directly associated with Tony Blair's vision of raising standards in schools by way of expanding self-governing trust schools and loosening the historic and traditional ties with the LEA.

It is instructive, however, to review the proposed legislation in terms of its alignment with the *Every Child Matters* agenda (as outlined in Chapter 2). In fact, the Bill echoes the rhetoric of the Children Act 2004 by placing a new duty on local authorities to promote *the fulfillment by every child concerned of his educational potential*. That said, the Education and Inspections Bill 2006 merely requires schools to *have regard* to local children and young people's plans (CYPPs), whereas many children's organisations want it to be a requirement for schools to act in accordance with the plans and to *secure the five outcomes* of the Children Act 2004 for all.

Significantly, the Bill accords greater control to the school in terms of admissions procedures – which has been extensively reported as a contentious issue. However, and of equal or even greater significance to children, young people and their families and carers on the margins of mainstream education, are the Bill's pronouncements regarding issues of discipline and exclusions.

Teachers are to be empowered to confiscate items such as mobile phones or knives and to use *reasonable* force to intervene in fights. Furthermore, headteachers may require children to attend detention sessions at weekends and during school holidays, as well as at the end of the school day.

Excluded children are defined as the responsibility of their parents, who must supervise them for the first five days after their exclusion, after which the local authority is obliged to arrange alternative lessons.

The Bill also sits in harmony with the Children Act 2004 in terms of a number of measures: its commitment to assisting pupils to catch up; in providing educational and recreational opportunities out of school hours; in its commitment to nutritional standards for food and drink offered at school; and in terms of its policy of extending free transport to broaden choice and access for all (although the latter point is highly contentious in terms of its capacity to dissociate children from their local schools).

CHAPTER SUMMARY

The extent to which the Raising Standards in Schools agenda fits with the *Every Child Matters* and School Inclusion agenda remains to be seen, and this dynamic tension will be explored further in Chapter 10.

In Chapter 4 we will move beyond the realm of legislation, policies and procedures, and will examine why some children and young people become significantly disaffected and disengaged from the schools and education environment, to the extent that they become the subjects of concern for a range of family and carer members, and to professionals – including teachers, school support workers, education welfare officers, educational and child psychologists, and social workers. The question we will seek to address is: What is going on for these people in that school appears to have so little to offer?

FURTHER READING

Education and Inspections Bill 2006. London: The Stationery Office.

The White Paper: *Higher Standards, Better Schools for All*. London: The Stationery Office.

Brayne, H and Carr, H (2005) *Law for social workers*, 9th edition. Oxford: Oxford University Press.

Calman, T (2001) 'Special Educational Needs' in L.A. Cull and J. Roche (eds) *The law and social work*. Basingstoke: Palgrave.

Johns, R (2005) *Using the law in social work*, 2nd edition. Exeter: Learning Matters.

The above represent a useful and helpful range of texts for the practitioner to expand their knowledge of relevant and contextual legislation.

Chapter 4

School's out: Making sense of disaffection, absenteeism and exclusion

To me education is a leading out of what is already in that pupil's soul. To Miss Mackay it is a putting in of something that is not there, and that is not what I call education, I call it intrusion.
(Muriel Spark (1961) *The Prime of Miss Jean Brodie* chapter 2)

Soap and education are not as sudden as a massacre, but they are more deadly in the long run.
(Mark Twain (1872))

ACHIEVING A SOCIAL WORK DEGREE

This chapter will help you meet the following National Occupational Standards:
Key Role 2: Plan, carry out, review and evaluate social work practice, with individuals, families, carers, groups and communities:
- Interact to achieve change and development and to improve life opportunities.
- Prepare, produce, implement and evaluate plans.

Key Role 3: Support individuals to represent their needs, views and circumstances:
- Prepare for, and take part in, decision-making forums.

It will also introduce you to the following academic standards as set out in the social work subject benchmark statement:

3.1.1 Social work services and service users
- The social processes (associated with, for example, poverty, unemployment, poor health, disablement, lack of education and other sources of disadvantage) that lead to marginalisation, isolation and exclusion and their impact on the demand for social work services.
- The nature of social work services in a diverse society.
- The nature and validity of different definitions of, and explanations for, the characteristics and circumstances of service users and the service required by them.

3.1.3 Values and ethics
- The nature, historical evolution and application of social work values.
- Rights, responsibilities, freedom, authority and power in the practice of social workers as moral and statutory agents.
- Complex relationship of justice, care and control – practical and ethical implications.
- Conceptual links between codes of ethics, regulation of professional conduct and management of potential conflicts between codes of different professions.

3.1.4 Social work theory
- Research-based concepts and critical explanations from social work theory base of social work.

The scope of the problem

A cursory reading of social history would seem to suggest that every generation of *adults* seems fated to regarding its contemporary youth as more difficult, problematic and challenging than any that have preceded it, a phenomenon so pertinently analysed by Geoffrey Pearson, in the study of *Hooligan: A History of Respectable Fears* (1983). That said, the *moral panic* (Cohen, 1972) about non-school attendance, as we saw in Chapter 1, has a lengthy history (probably coterminous with the concept of compulsory education itself), and becomes most acute when it is causally linked to other political concerns, such as offending, anti-social behaviour, drug use, teenage pregnancy and general social exclusion. Thus those outside school – whether by virtue of truancy or exclusion – become seen as a homogeneous, threatening conglomerate and conform to Cohen's notion of the *moral panic* (1972, p9) when *a condition, episode, person or group emerges to become defined as a threat to societal values and interests*. Such a group invariably commands the intense, yet often transitory attention of politicians, the press, social and political commentators and moral theorists.

Indeed, as noted by Wright *et al* (2000, p26), there emerges a particular desire to control and amend the behaviour of a specific group: ... *the challenging few have become a group of individuals likely not only to damage the educational chances of other more well behaved pupils, but in doing so they are seen as adversely affecting the ability of the school to attract more desirable pupils.*

Therefore, the Government sees reducing absence from school as a priority because of the perceived strong link between school attendance and attainment, and also because of the links between truancy and street crime and general anti-social behaviour. As a result of these assumptions, the New Labour Government has made school attendance a key plank of its social inclusion agenda.

As Tony Blair (quoted in Jeffs and Smith, 2002, p3) has stated: *The best defence against social exclusion is having a job, and the best way to get a job is to have a good education* and the presumed starting point for having a *good* education is attendance.

So, what is the nature of the extent of *the problem*? Or more correctly, what is the extent of this *set of alleged problems*? Are children and young people any more disaffected from education and schooling than they have been before? Or is it just the case that our society has become progressively less tolerant of difference?

Absenteeism and truancy

How many children and young people are not in school at any one time?

According to an earlier survey by O'Keefe in 1994 (cited in Newburn and Shiner, 2005, p11), *almost one third of pupils truant at sometime, and over 8% truant at least once a week (rising to one in ten in Year II)*. Historically, a distinction was made between authorised absence – which accounts for the vast majority of the missed days – and unauthorised absence, which was defined, by default, as truancy. Because of the alleged links between *truancy* and its associated *public ills*, such as youth offending and public disorder, the traditional focus has been on unauthorised absenteeism. In 1996–97, unauthorised absences were at the level of 0.7 per cent, rising to 0.71 per cent (with junior school levels at 0.43 per cent and the rate for secondary schools being 1.08 per cent) in 2002–03 (Department for Education and Skills (DfES), 2003a) and rising to an overall figure of 0.79 per cent in 2004–05. In essence, this amounts to children and young people missing 2,270,000 days of primary school education and 5,685,000 days of secondary education as a result of unauthorised absence.

However, such a distinction between authorised and unauthorised has now been abandoned, in favour of addressing overall attendance figures. By focusing on absence as a whole, the government has been able to claim that overall absence rates have reduced from 7.23 per cent of half days in 1996–97 to 6.45 per cent in 2004–05 – a change equivalent to an extra 50,000 pupils regularly attending school every day.

However, it is reluctantly acknowledged that the underlying level of persistent disaffection and absence has been little affected by the raft of initiatives introduced in recent years, and Jacqui Smith (the Schools Minister) lamented that *it is disappointing that a stubborn minority of pupils in just 4% of secondary schools, remain determined to jeopardise their education and their futures through persistent truancy.* The Minister announced that 146 secondary schools, accounting for one in five of all instances of truancy, must identify their 8,000 most persistent truants, and put their parents on the fast track to attendance scheme (see Chapter 5).

In summary, current official figures (DfES, 2005a) state that, on average, 450,000 children are absent from school every day including 50,000 unauthorised absences. Significantly, 29 per cent of persistent truants leave school with no qualifications, compared with 2 per cent of non-truants. In other words, and as you would expect, the truism that *you have to be there to get the prizes* holds up to scrutiny.

In Chapter 5, we will further examine the range of legal and practice interventions available as a response to this issue, and which we introduced in Chapter 3, but we need to begin by thinking about how we make sense of any social phenomena, such as school absence. This takes us into the realm of theorising, which should underpin all social work and social care practice. Furthermore, it is of particular value to reflect upon our own experiences of schooling in terms of attendance and absence, as a tool towards understanding the actions of another person.

ACTIVITY **4.1**

This is an activity to do with someone you trust in terms of personal information. Try to answer the questions as honestly as you can. The questions to be considered are:

- *Did you ever miss any days (or part days) whilst at school, and if so, why?*

- *And, of equal importance: if you never missed a day at school, why not?*

- *If you were absent, what slang term did you call your absence in your home area?*

Your answers

Comment

Of course, it is highly unlikely that you attended every day of your schooling. At one end of the spectrum are those absences seen as inevitable, as *blameless*. You will probably not have even mentioned these crosses on the register, which will largely have been accounted for in terms of illnesses, or hospital appointments, or family difficulties, sorrows, celebrations and events (such as weddings, graduations, births and funerals), or transitions such as moving house and moving schools. Most of these absences will have been *authorised* in that the school will have been informed of them by your parent(s) or carer(s), or the school would have been happy to note them down as authorised, albeit retrospectively.

However, next on the spectrum comes that fuzzy, middle or grey area – of holidays taken in term time, of visits to relatives, of having a day off for your birthday, or your brother's birthday, or the *I didn't feel like going* category – all conducted with or without the knowledge or permission or your parent or carer.

Finally, comes the clearer territory of knowing and conscious absenteeism and the language used to describe such behaviour – what you might have referred to as *playing truant*, *skipping off*, *bunking off*, *mitching*, *dodging*, *skiving*, *going missing* or *playing hookey*. As Reid (2000, p1) notes, many of these terms are associated with fun, with playing, and with the inherent notion of the free spirited child defeating the best intentions of the controlling adult world. In this sense, the *truant* becomes an heroic figure, like *Tom Sawyer*, attempting to resist the dead hand of formal lessons by *learning* in the real world, by going fishing or such like. We need to acknowledge that our society, like many others in the advanced capitalist West, has a long, complex and ambivalent attitude towards the compulsory nature of education, and towards formal schooling itself.

So, how do *you* make sense of children and young people not attending school?

ACTIVITY 4.2

*Every person on the proverbial Clapham Omnibus has an idea about why certain young people do not attend school. What might these common sense explanations be? You might find it helpful to think in terms of a force field analysis – what factors **push** children and young people out of school, and what factors **pull** them out of school. Try to note down your first six thoughts, three for each side of the force field:*

Push factors (pushing children out of school):

1.

2.

3.

Pull factors (pulling children out of school):

1.

2.

3.

Comment

In attempting this exercise, you might have thought of factors that match some of the points below:

1. *Push-factor 1: the school informally excludes various children.*

2. *Push-factor 2: the child is bullied at school.*

3. *Push-factor 3: the education on offer is not appropriate to some children.*

4. *Push-factor 4: the child has experienced negative schooling in the past.*

5. *Push-factor 5: there is non-identification of child's additional needs.*

6. *Pull-factor 1: education is devalued by parents/carers.*

7. *Pull-factor 2: parents actively keep children out of school.*

8. *Pull-factor 3: the child stays at home to care for/protect another family member.*

9. *Pull-factor 4: the young person is subject to peer pressure to stay out of school.*

Offering another way of thinking about the issue, The NFER study of 1997, cited in Youth Justice Board (2003a, p25) categorised pupils' views on school absence as follows:

- **Influence of friends and peers:** Some people think if my mates can do it, I can do it ... they don't want to feel left out.

- **Relationships with teachers:** It's the teachers that cause truancy – not so much the work because the work's usually OK. The teachers' attitude to you, the way they talk down at you – they've got no right.

- **Content and delivery of the curriculum:** ... sometimes, I just bunked off lessons because I thought 'Oh God, it's science, and I don't want to do science'.

- **Family factors:** ... Mum used to make me stay at home, because my dad, he used to hit her, and she said 'you'll have to stay at home in case he comes back' and I just stayed at home because I felt right horrible if I came to school.

- **Bullying:** I didn't like school, and sometimes it was because of the other people cussing me or something, and getting me upset.

- **Classroom context:** When I didn't understand a bit of work, the teachers never used to bother, so I thought 'sod it, if they ain't going to help me, I ain't going to help myself, I'm not going to school'.

These findings are borne out by recent research (Malcolm *et al*, 2003), with parents seeing the main causes of truancy as bullying, problems with teachers and peer pressure to stay away from school. Secondary school pupils are more likely to attribute their absence from school to school-related factors rather than home-related factors. These reasons include problems with lessons, problems with teachers, being bullied, peer pressure and social isolation.

As before, we can see these processes in terms of *push/pull* dynamics – factors pushing the child out of the school, or factors pulling the child out. To take this further, we will consider another way of thinking about the triangular relationship between the child (or young person), the parent or carer, and the school.

According to the assessment framework developed by MacDonald and Daly (1996, pp14–19), there are three main players in the game, namely the *child*, the *parent* and the *school community*. All three of these players can exhibit enabling behaviours which make school attendance and engagement more likely – and similarly all three can exhibit inhibiting behaviour which conversely make school attendance and engagement less likely.

It is worth noting that this is a systems-based or ecological approach, and recognises that all three elements are interconnected, and indeed are interdependent. In that sense, it mirrors and reflects the assessment triangle – the child, the family and the environment – that was introduced via the Framework for the Assessment of Children and Their Needs (Department of Health/ DfEE/ Home Office, 2000).

ACTIVITY 4.3

Think of a particular child, family/carer and school, based upon your own experience of professional practice. Try to identify the following:

- *Child behaviour which enhances school attendance:*

- *Parental behaviour which enhances school attendance:*

- *School behaviour which enhances school attendance:*

Conversely, the same three players can exhibit disabling behaviours. As above, try to identify the following:

- *Child behaviour which inhibits school attendance:*

- *Parental behaviour which inhibits school attendance:*

- *School behaviour which inhibits school attendance:*

Models of explanation

According to Hoyle (1998, p100) broad themes have been consistently present in the literature of truancy for over a century to explain absence, which is largely seen as a consequence of the individual pathologies of *incompetent* parents, feckless deviants, or children who experience anxiety discords because of schooling.

Furthermore, research by Hoyle (1998, p107) identifies three diagnostic categories being used to informally *sort* school absentees, in descending order of offending:

(1) *truant* – a deviant from a deviant family or community; exhibiting willful absence;

(2) *school refuser* – a child who is conceived of as 'half bad and half good'; refusing to attend due to experiences of abuse, neglect, poverty; and

(3) *school phobic* – a child with mental health difficulties, enmeshed with parents/carers, unable to take advantage of the school opportunities.

Such a typology has echoes with Packman's defining characterisation of children in public care as being defined as *mad*, *bad* or *sad* (Packman, 1985).

Whilst the tolerance of school absence due to the adverse conditions of the middle ground has lessened, in accordance with the philosophy of *No More Excuses* as applied by the Home Office (1997) to youth offending, the diversity of reasons that explain school *phobia* and the behaviour problems associated with problematic schooling have multiplied.

Before we explore these difficulties, let us also consider truancy alongside other associated issues of underachievement and disruptive behaviour, as shown on the bottom row:

Children and young people of compulsory school age (5–16)		
Those who do well at school – who attend, who engage and who achieve		
Those who just about cope in school – with specialist and targeted support		
Those who are absent	Those who are underachieving	Those who are disruptive

Figure 4.1 *Absence, underachievement and disruption*

These are by no means mutually exclusive groups, and young people often move between the three categories on the bottom line, and many indeed have periodic episodes of functioning in the middle or even top rows. Nevertheless, the chances are that if children and young people spend a significant period of time being characterised as absent, underachieving or disruptive, then it is highly likely they will also become the object of government concern, even when beyond the age of compulsory education.

As we will show in the next few sections, once young people become locked into the bottom line, then whether they become absent, or end up excluded, is at once random and yet also determined by the person's gender, ethnicity and culture.

Associated difficulties: the example of ADHD

Disaffection can have a myriad of explanations and causations, many of which are exclusively the domain of socio-political enquiry, but a significant cluster of difficulties that straddles the contested arena of biology, developmental psychology and culture is associated with the broad term of *conduct disorders*. For the purposes of illustration, we will explore one such defined phenomena, that of attention deficit hyperactive disorder (ADHD).

Children and young people experiencing ADHD usually have three main kinds of problems:

(1) overactive behaviour (hyperactivity);

(2) impulsive behaviour;

(3) difficulty in paying attention.

Some children only have the last of these and they are described as having attention deficit disorder (ADD), with the associate difficulties of hyperactivity and impulsiveness.

The following quote illustrates the difficulties and stresses of caring for a child with ADHD symptoms:

> *The day always began from the moment he was awake with his exhausting and insatiable demands. No one was prepared to babysit because he was so exhausting and a liability. It was impossible to enjoy him and no fun to take him anywhere. His energy levels were incredible. As parents we wondered where we were going wrong.*
>
> (Alison Douglas, *Young Minds*, p39, cited by Mental Health Foundation (2006))

In terms of epidemiology, about 0.5–1 per cent of children in the UK are thought to have attention or hyperactivity problems, although the USA has produced figures of 10 per cent using much broader definitions. About five times more boys than girls are diagnosed, and there are over representations of particular ethnic groups, such as for African-Caribbean boys.

It is highly unlikely that ADHD is a new phenomenon, unless associated, as had been thought at first, with particular societal changes in diet and the advent of food additives. It is more likely that in previous generations hyperactive behaviour was physically punished in schools, or such children were allowed to leave education altogether. In other words, the advancement of routine measurement and testing, the National Tests process and the replacement of punishment with diagnosis have all lead to heightened levels of problem identification. In fact, not surprisingly, research suggests that 90 per cent of children with ADHD underachieve at school and 20 per cent have reading difficulties.

Whilst medication has been used with varying levels of success as a means to modify ADHD, both parents and schools have implemented effective behaviour management programmes, coupled with experimentations with diet.

Children and young people with behavioural difficulties are, inevitably, at risk of exclusions from school. This needs to be explored and explained.

School exclusions – fixed term and permanent

According to Wrigley (2003, p162) *(t)he introduction of market competition between schools in England lead to a 450% increase in the number of permanent exclusions between 1990 and 1995*. This significant development disproportionately impacts upon specific groups of vulnerable children and young people: those with behavioural difficulties and learning difficulties; boys in secondary school, and particularly those of African-Caribbean heritage; and those who are looked after (Blyth and Milner, 1996). Furthermore, it indicates a shift in the social construction of problems, rather than a change in the nature of behaviour itself. As Mittler (2000, p63) suggests, whilst the incidence of emotional behavioural disorders has changed very little in recent decades, *(w)hat has changed is the tolerance levels of the schools to pupils with disruptive behaviour*. We will look firstly at the modes of exclusions and then consider some of the themes and trends associated with this highly contentious, but significant phenomenon.

The law allows pupils to be excluded for a total of 45 days in any school year and there are two types of exclusion.

Fixed-term exclusion:

The exclusion should be for the shortest possible time. If the exclusion period is to be for more that 15 days, then the local education authority (LEA) is required to arrange full-time education for the pupil. In 2003–04, nearly 350,000 children were excluded for fixed terms.

Permanent exclusion

Following a permanent exclusion, there is a duty upon the LEA to provide suitable, alternative education.

Let us look at some statistics first, examining the scope of the exclusion phenomena, and the characteristics of those who are excluded:

- 9,980 pupils in England were permanently excluded in 2003–04 (an increase of 6 per cent on the previous year and compared with 9,540 in 2001–02).

- Boys are four times more likely to be excluded than girls (82 per cent of excluded pupils were boys, and the most common age is 13–14).

- Amongst Asian pupils, boys are 10 times more likely to be excluded than girls.

- Black Caribbean children are three times as likely to be excluded as white children or black African pupils. (In 1998–99, 60 out of every 10,000 black Caribbean pupils were excluded) (DfES, 2003c).

- In 2001–02, 41 in every 10,000 black Caribbean pupils were permanently excluded, compared with only 2 in every 10,000 Chinese pupils – the lowest rate.

- Pupils from traveller communities are four times more likely to be excluded than other students.

- Some studies have suggested that between 20–25 per cent of permanently excluded pupils are looked after by the local authority.

A study by the Children's Society (Hayden and Dunne, quoted by Hendrick, 2003, p219) revealed that *boys are 10 times more likely to be excluded than girls at primary schools and four times more likely at secondary school; black children are six times more likely to be excluded than white children; children with special needs are seven times more likely to be excluded than any other group.*

So, what are the reasons as to why children and young people are excluded?

We have seen that some groups experience higher levels of vulnerability to exclusion than others. How do we make sense of this? Note down your thoughts.

Comment

You might have noted some of the following factors. The most commonly stated reason for exclusion is persistent disruptive behaviour, which accounts for 20 per cent of the figure (*SocietyGuardian*, 2005, p76) although bullying is also one of the most common reasons for schools excluding young people (Hyams-Parish, 1995). It is inevitable that as concern for the bullied victim has increased, so the authority's reaction by excluding the perpetrator has become more likely. It is important to note, in spite of media portrayals to the contrary, that only 1 per cent of exclusions arise from physical abuse and assaults upon staff, whilst 30 per cent are for bullying, fighting and assaults upon peers.

Research by Parsons and Howlett (2000) shows that a third of children excluded from primary schools and two thirds of those excluded from secondary schools never return to mainstream education – thus we have the spectre of a *de facto* permanently excluded group destined to join the not currently engaged in employment, education, or training (NEET) statistics (see Figure 4.2 below).

Of course, every child or young person is unique with specific issues and circumstances, but the research evidence points to significant trends and to representations of disaffection in specific population groups.

Problematised progression outcomes: Post-16

Whatever the reasons, the fact is that 1 in 11 young people aged between 16 and 18 are not in education, employment or training, and alongside Greece and Portugal, the UK has the lowest number of 18-year-olds in education in the EU.

Young people of post compulsory school age (16+)		
Those not in education	Those not in employment	Those not in training

Figure 4.2 *NEET – not in education, employment or training*

According to government policy, this really matters because: *Ensuring young people are in full time education, training or employment is the single most important factor in reducing the risk of youth offending ...* (Youth Justice Board, 2003b, p16).

According to the DfES (2002), 25 per cent of all young people aged 16 have no GCSE passes at grade A to C, and 5 per cent of boys and 4 per cent of girls have no GCSE passes at any grade. In 2000, one in four 16–18 year olds in Britain had dropped out of education and training – in terms of the OECD and EU, Britain came 25th out of 29 countries. Britain is notable for low status accorded to vocational study and for the segregated nature of post-16 work.

If we accept that this is a problem, and the nature of defining problems is, by its very nature, a contested process, then how do we explain this pattern of persistent disaffection and underachievement for a small but significant group of young people?

Explaining education difficulty

As GCSE passes at grade C and above have emerged as the benchmark for being engaged and successful, and result in the transition towards education, employment or further training, then those unable, unwilling or unsupported to follow suit have become progressively isolated and disaffected, in actual and relative terms. As Bentley and Gurumurthy (1999, cited in Newburn and Shiner, 2005, p28) suggest *while many are achieving more than their parents' generation, for others the choices and risks have become more stark ... those who have not kept pace with this trend (towards increased achievement) are relatively more disadvantaged.*

This is a critical point. Only a generation ago, the British *norm* was to leave school at the minimum age (then 15, rising to 16) with few or minimal qualifications, and to join a diverse labour market that could absorb essentially unqualified or poorly qualified entrants, and which was prepared to train people *on-the-job*, through various *time-serving* or apprenticeship processes. In other words, school was something to suffer, to survive and proceeed through, but it was not the key determinant of a young person's future. In many communities, progression for young males into traditional occupations (such as mining, shipbuilding, heavy engineering, farming) had nothing to do with educational achievements and outcomes. However, rising standards (meaning higher levels of attainment) now mean that opportunities are reduced for those outside the performance norm.

In one sense, such changes have disproportionately affected young males in an adverse manner. Although Douglas (in 1964) was showing that girls were outperforming boys in primary schools, the current concern about *boys' underachievement* has assumed the status of a moral panic (Wrigley, 2003, p168) and this aspect of educational *under performance* is directly linked to associated risk factors for male *failure* – excessive substance use/misuse, offending behaviour, public disorder, imprisonment, lack of self respect and respect for others, mental ill health, self harm and suicide.

The changing labour market, linked to qualifications thresholds, can be portrayed as follows (see Figure 4.3), to indicate the reduced opportunities for those who *miss out* at school:

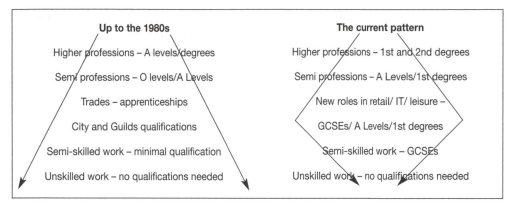

Figure 4.3 *Labour market changes: Employment opportunities*

The changing pattern – from the pyramid to the diamond – means that the opportunities for the majority are now determined by GCSE, A Level and undergraduate degree achievements. Such a change in the market means that the price of not succeeding at school is relatively much higher than it has been in the recent past, and some families have struggled to acknowledge the need to convey different messages about the meaning and value of education to their offspring. The following quote represents a critical and apparently unsympathetic view of parents who *fail* to endorse educational achievement, but it serves to illustrate the importance attributed to parental and kinship values:

> *Parents of the manual occupational groups show signs of disaffection from the schools their children attend ... they provide the weakest educational support for their children ... their homes show the least evidence of literacy ... some of these parents' other attitudes are out of step with those of the school ...*
> (J.M. Brynner, quoted in Holland, 1992, p67).

The recent research evidence reinforces the view of family values as a significant determinant of educational engagement – or conversely of disaffection. According to Newburn and Shiner (2005, p13) ... *the odds of a young person from a low-skilled family engaging in a high level of truancy are 80 per cent higher than for a person from professional or managerial family*, and the research seems to indicate that whilst literacy and numeracy strategies have helped marginal children, pupils in the most deprived areas have been falling, relatively, further behind over the past ten years. Furthermore, families with differing and diverse cultural values will generate differing reactions to expressions of general school-based disaffection, and according to Sasson (1993, p11): *When white youngsters are turned off by schools and the curriculum, they truant. Black youngsters are forced by their parents to go to school, where they become disruptive and in due course expelled.*

Some or all of these models of explanation may be relevant. The individual practitioner, when undertaking an assessment, needs to be aware that their own personal values and experiences will lead them into emphasising some models over others. We also need to be constantly aware of our own perspectives – in terms of age, gender, race, ethnicity, sexuality and disabilities – as determinants of what we choose to include and exclude from the assessment framework. We need to be constantly aware of our potential to stereotype and label people (Milner and O'Byrne, 2002). We also need to be able to see things from different perspectives.

C H A P T E R   S U M M A R Y

In this chapter, we have attempted to begin to understand various ways of thinking about school disaffection, absenteeism, underachievement and social exclusion. There seems to be little doubt that whilst children and young people bring into the school milieu different forms of social and cultural capital, based upon their race, ethnicity, gender, class, history, upbringing, the current school improvement agenda is having differential impacts on particular groups within total pupil population. The following quote from Fullan encapsulates the tensions between *whole school* objectives and the demands of devising a regime best suited to those least able to take advantage of the *improving* school:

> *... the greater the emphasis on academic achievement through high stakes accountability, the greater the gap become between advantaged and disadvantaged students. The main reason for this is that poor performing students do not need more pressure; they need greater attachment to school and motivation to want to learn. Pressure by itself in this situation actually demotivates poor performing students.*
> (Fullan, 1999)

We have already looked at the broad legal options in Chapter 3. However, in acknowledging that the legal framework is highly significant, we are interested in beginning to look at ways of working with disaffected children and young people. We will begin by examining the role of the education welfare service, which has historically been charged with the task of addressing issues of absenteeism, truancy, disaffection and exclusion.

FURTHER READING

Malcolm, H, Wilson, V, Davidson, J and Kirk, S (2003) *Absence from School: A Study of its Causes and Effects in Seven LEAs*. Nottingham: NFER/DfES.

A thorough examination of persistent absence from school.

Munn, P, Lloyd, G and Cullen, AM (2000) *Alternatives to exclusion from school*. London: Paul Chapman.

A really helpful text that offers ways of thinking about disaffected behaviour in education settings.

Chapter 5

School's in: Addressing particular issues

Children are not born good … they have to be disciplined, otherwise they're a threat to the rest of society.
(Dr Rhodes Boyson (cited in Holland, 1992, p60))

New Labour has set out a new authoritarian approach towards non-school attendance and truancy.
(Grier and Thomas (2005, p133))

Special needs … those needs to which schools currently do not respond.
(Booth, 1983, p7)

ACHIEVING A SOCIAL WORK DEGREE

This chapter will help you meet the following National Occupational Standards:

Key Role 1: Prepare for and work with individuals, families, carers, groups and communities to assess their needs and circumstances:
- Prepare for social work contact and involvement.
- Work with individuals, families, carers, groups and communities to help them make informed decisions.
- Assess needs and options to recommend a course of action.

Key Role 2: Plan, carry out, review and evaluate social work practice, with individuals, families, carers, groups, communities and other professionals:
- Interact with individuals, families, carers, groups and communities to achieve change and development and to improve life opportunities.
- Prepare, produce, implement and evaluate plans.

Key Role 3: Support individuals to represent their needs, views and circumstances:
- Prepare for, and take part in, decision-making forums.

It will also introduce you to the following academic standards as set out in the social work subject benchmark statement:

3.1.1 Social work services and service users
- The relationship between agency policies, legal requirements and professional boundaries in shaping the nature of services provided in multi-disciplinary contexts and the issues associated with working across professional boundaries and within inter-disciplinary groups.

5.1.2 Ability to use this knowledge and understanding in work within specific practice settings

The business of education welfare provision

Education welfare officers (EWOs) are clearly a vital cog in the children's services wheel, but what do they actually do? The London Borough of Brent has published a Service Statement, which helpfully summarises the core objectives:

> *Education welfare officers are responsible for helping parents to ensure that their children of school age attend school regularly. EWOs have a duty to promote and secure high levels of school attendance. They visit schools regularly to consult with teachers and check attendance registers. They also provide advice and support on areas such as bullying, exclusion, alternative education provision, child protection and behaviour difficulties.*

The scope of education welfare practice

According to Lyons (2002), EWOs are engaged in the following core issues: attendance, truancy and exclusions; youth employment; child protection and schools; the education of children with *special educational needs* (SENs); and education of children looked after by local authorities. However, as the author notes, *social work in relation to schools in the United Kingdom, as provided in the education welfare service, has a long history but an ambiguous position structurally in relation to both education and the personal social services* (Lyons, 2002, p212).

The Government has, for a number of years, been reviewing the optimum organisational location of EWOs, as evidenced by Jacqui Smith's statement of 2001:

> *Education welfare officers have a long history of working directly with school and families to promote regular attendance. We are currently piloting whether EWOs employed directly by schools would help to improve this liaison and assist in our overall aim of reducing the number of school truancies.*

Varying responsibilities depend upon the specific local education authority (LEA): some services have responsibility for excluded pupils, for missing children, for education-related benefits such as assistance with school clothing, free school meals and school transport, and for the monitoring of home-educated pupils. The following list begins to summarise the work undertaken by education welfare services:

> ### The scope of the education welfare service
>
> - *accept and act upon referrals of pupils who are failing to attend school regularly;*
>
> - *provide casework support and assistance to pupils and families in resolving issues that prevent a young person gaining maximum benefit from their education;*
>
> - *where appropriate, seek to apply legal sanctions in the magistrates' court against parents who fail to send their children to school regularly or to use the various legal options as outlined in Chapter 3;*
>
> - *support and challenge schools in the effective management of attendance and absence;*
>
> - *work in partnership with other agencies to promote regular school attendance;*
>
> - *in partnership with the police and other agencies, to conduct truancy sweeps;*
>
> - *in summary, Blyth (2000, p108) asserts that the aim of education social work is to ensure that children obtain optimum benefit from a meaningful educational experience.*

The organisation of school enforcement

Although linked to the very beginnings of State intervention in school provision, school attendance enforcement had no national framework, and was organised at a local level. The education welfare service (EWS) is not a statutory function: there is no legal requirement for LEAs to have an EWS, although the LEA has to exercise its legal duties under section 437 of the Education Act 1996 through some form of service or agency. There has never been a national pay or professional structure, but in the early years a recognition of the parallels with social work lead to an alignment with social work training and qualifications, resulting in some LEAs employing educational social workers, or social workers in education.

Although the service itself is not a statutory one, each LEA has to devise strategies for discharging its duties and responsibilities for ensuring school attendance, for monitoring and regulating child employment, and these duties have traditionally been discharged by the EWS.

The following are key drivers that shape the EWS and how it and the LEA manage attendance and absence:

- *National, LEA and school level targets to reduce truancy and exclusion*: the current public service agreement in relation to school absence is to reduce the 2003 level by 8 per cent by the year 2008.

- *Legislation*: Children Act 1989, Education Act 1996, Crime and Disorder Act 1998, Police and Criminal Evidence Act 1984, Anti-social Behaviour Act 2003, Pupil Registration Regulations 1995.

- *New powers for LEAs, the police, local authorities and schools*: these include truancy sweeps, penalty notices, clear links with anti-social behaviour strategies and fast-track legal proceedings.

- *Parental responsibility*: parenting orders, parenting contracts, increased legal sanctions for parents who fail to fulfill their legal responsibilities.

- *Government guidance*: Circulars 10/99 and 11/99.

- *Emphasis on the needs of vulnerable groups*: travellers, looked after children, pregnant school pupils, pupils with long-term illness.

- *Well-defined expectations*: from the DfES, the National Audit Office, and the Office for Standards in Education (Ofsted), on minimum LEA and schools standards and actions to address absence from school.

- *Raised national awareness*: about the importance of educational attendance, achievement, outcomes and qualifications.

- *National Occupational Standards for the service*.

These objectives may be achieved by delivering services in the following ways:

- area or patch-based teams;

- school-based;

- within multi-agency teams.

EWOs should build an effective working relationship with schools to resolve attendance problems by:

- working closely with schools to define their role and responsibilities surrounding school attendance;

- defining the EWS's roles and responsibilities;

- ensuring that policies and operational practices are shared between the EWS and schools;

- agreeing arrangements for referral, regular review, monitoring and evaluation;

- agreeing procedures for resolving enquiries.

The LEA must work with schools to ensure that attendance registers are kept up-to-date and are accurately completed. Where legal action is taken against the parent, the court can consider only unauthorised absence because, by definition, any authorised absence has already been approved by the school.

The LEA should set out the amount of support that schools can expect from the EWS. The support should be based on clear and straightforward criteria. Any formula for EWS resource allocation should take into account the extent of absence from school and the number of pupils on the school roll.

Each school maintained by the LEA should have a named EWO who is responsible for liaison with the school. LEAs should monitor carefully the use of all different types of intervention strategies to assess whether they are effective and appropriate.

When a case is referred to the LEA, the EWO should make an assessment of the case and work closely with the pupil and their family as well as the school to resolve issues surrounding their poor attendance. This may involve making home visits and securing a problem-solving dialogue between home and school.

The EWS should consider and attempt to resolve any possible factors that may be contributing to school attendance problems. Documentary evidence should be kept to prove that the EWO has undertaken casework to address possible reasons for non-attendance. This should include evidence of action taken by the school.

There are a number of individuals and organisations that may be able to assist in various ways with resolving poor attendance problems. These include educational psychologists, health workers, social work practitioners in children's services, child and adolescent mental health services (CAMHS), Connexions, SEN Co-ordinators (SENCOs), youth offending teams (YOTs), behaviour and education support teams (BESTs), multi-agency support teams (MASTs) and the police. This list is not exhaustive and schools and local authorities should endeavour to make links with all relevant organisations in their area.

Practice issues: Fast track to prosecution for school absence

The Fast Track to Prosecution Framework began in January 2003 and by June 2004 was being implemented in more than two thirds of LEAs. Parents placed on the scheme must improve their child's school attendance over a 12-week period or face prosecution, normally resulting in a fine of up to £2,500 or three months' imprisonment. However, the scheme is not without its critics. Jacqui Newvell, head of the National Children's Bureau's pupil inclusion unit suggests that: *We have to recognize that in many families where truancy is persistent, parents may already be struggling to cope and punitive measures will only make things worse* (quoted in *Children Now*, 11–17 January 2006).

Nevertheless, the then Minister said the Government was committed to *sanctions such as prosecution and penalty fines for those parents who are simply unwilling to get their children to school*. The Government wants the parents of persistent truants to be placed on the Fast Track to Attendance Scheme, which results in a fine or imprisonment if a child's attendance does not improve within 12 weeks.

Overall, about 7,500 parents are taken to court each year in relation to their child's lack of education (by school attendance or otherwise), although only a handful of those ever receive a custodial sentence.

Truancy sweeps

Introduced by the Government in 2002 these are carried out by police officers and EWOs, under the powers of section 16 of the Crime and Disorder Act of 1998 (DfES, 2002b). The police have power to pick up (but not arrest) children suspected of playing truant, and to take them to a designated suitable place, or back to school. The truancy sweep teams focus their activities on particular areas, such as shopping centres. Conducted at least twice a year, data from previous *sweeps* shows that 46.5 per cent of *truants* were in fact with an adult (who is therefore colluding with the child's absence from school).

A comprehensive study by Halsey *et al* (2003) of such sweeps in seven LEAs indicated that the best results, on the day, arose from a non-confrontational approach with low-profile police presence. The study also affirmed the importance of involvement in schools in the activity, and of follow-up strategies to engage with those caught in the *sweep*.

Further research evidence from various studies prior to the introduction of the truancy sweep policy appeared to attest to their efficacy. The Social Exclusion Unit (2001) claimed that truancy patrols in York in 1999 coincided with reductions in crime of 67 per cent on the day, and in Newham, London with car crime being reduced by 70 per cent. However, the sweeps are periodic events, and may have the greatest effect in terms of raising awareness.

Bullying and anti-bullying strategies

Bullying is a complex and emotive phenomenon that occurs, to some degree, in every school and affects almost every child – directly or indirectly – at some stage of their educational career. The Children's Commissioner for England, Al Aynsley-Green has stated that … *Bullying is the most important issue that every child I meet is asking me to stamp out now*, and suggested in 2005 that pupils should be issued with end-of-term questionnaires to ascertain the extent of bullying in any particular school environment. Despite the prevalence of bullying in UK schools, preventing and addressing it when it occurs poses a significant challenge for teachers and others within the children's services arena. The perceived commodification of schools as marketable entities within a competitive local environment can in fact lead to the denial of bullying as an issue present within a particular locality, or to the failure to acknowledge bullying as a phenomenon that is, in fact, being vigorously addressed. This is understandable, as a school that is perceived to contain bullying behaviour will draw a significant amount of negative media interest, rather than being lauded for its honest and engaging actions. Of central importance to tackling bullying is an understanding of its impact on young people. Despite schools' assertions to the contrary, the experiences of pupils demonstrate that bullying is a major contributor to absence from school (as noted in Chapter 4), causing high levels of in-school truancy and having a significant impact on a young person's ability to gain the maximum benefit from their education. Victims of bullying may find the thought of going to school to be so terrifying that they feign illness or refuse to attend. The long-term effects of bullying can be devastating for the victim and, as the tragic cases reported in the media remind us, can lead to self-harm and even suicide. Bullying continues to be the single most common reason for children seeking help from ChildLine, accounting for about a quarter of all calls received. *The charity set out to uncover why, despite the mandatory introduction of anti-bullying policies by schools, ChildLine still speaks to around 20,000 children every year whose lives are made miserable because they are being bullied* (**www.teachernet.gov.uk**).

The resulting research, *Tackling Bullying: Listening to the Views of Children and Young People* (Oliver and Candappa, 2003) – a report commissioned by the DfES and undertaken by ChildLine – showed that over half of all secondary (54 per cent) and primary (51 per cent) thought that bullying was a *big problem* or *quite a problem* in their school. Over 60 per cent of pupils in both age groups felt that their school was *very good* or *quite good* at dealing with the problem. However, some schools were believed to fare better than others in tackling bullying.

Finding an appropriate and all-encompassing definition of bullying inevitably proves to be difficult. Bullying comprises a wide range of behaviours and consequences and the definition will vary from one expert to another whilst young people will have their own diverse opinions of what constitutes bullying. However, the following definitions perhaps go further than most in capturing the ingredients that characterise this complex issue:

> *Bullying is the willful, conscious desire to hurt or threaten or frighten someone else. To do this, the bully has to have some sort of power over the victim, a power not always recognisable to the teacher.*
> (Johnstone, Munn and Edwards, 1992, p3)

> *Bullying is the behaviour of one person or a group which causes distress to another person or group as a result of physical threat, assault, verbal abuse or threats.*
> *(Support Force for Residential Child Care, 1996, p3)*

Twenty years ago there were few examples of literature or research on bullying, but in recent years there has been a wealth of studies on the subject and schools can draw good practice guidance from a range of sources, including the DfES. Similarly, organisations such as ACE, Kidscape, The Anti-Bullying Alliance and the Children's Legal Centre provide information and guidance for professionals and for parents.

Bullying: The Government's response

Whilst the Government agenda for schools has focused on achievement, truancy, and league tables, parents place great importance on the safety and happiness of their child during the time they are in school. Recent government legislation has focused sharply on reinforcing parental responsibility and on giving teachers a mandate to challenge poor behaviour in the classroom. On 21 November 2005, at the start of the second annual anti-bullying week, Jacqui Smith reaffirmed the Government's White Paper commitment to establishing measures to tackle bullying and all forms of bad behaviour, including:

- a legal right for teachers to discipline pupils, strengthening their authority, and giving them the confidence to take firm action on all forms of bad behaviour;

- giving schools the power to apply for court-imposed parenting orders to compel the parents of bullying or badly behaved children to attend parenting classes or face £1,000 fines;

- making parents take responsibility for excluded pupils in the first five days of a suspension;

- new powers for head teachers to search pupils for knives and other sharp weapons through the Violent Crime Reduction Bill;

- school partnerships sharing off-site learning support units for badly behaved pupils, with the first expected to be operational in the new year.

In making judgements on personal development and well-being, Ofsted inspections now assess the levels of bullying in schools and seek the views of pupils and parents to ensure it is being tackled effectively.

What are schools required to do?

It is compulsory for schools to have policies in place to prevent and tackle bullying. Governors and staff have a legal duty to publish a written policy on pupil behaviour and discipline. The policy should include clear statements about bullying and should state that it will not be tolerated and that firm action will be taken if, and when, incidents occur.

The policy should be brought to the attention of and should be accessible to all staff, governors, pupils and their parents. Furthermore, a procedure for reporting and recording bullying behaviour should be established and detailed in the policy. Finally, some definitions and examples of bullying behaviour should also be given to pupils and parents so that they can identify and respond to incidents when they occur.

The challenge for schools

Having a policy and a clear continuum of sanctions will ensure schools satisfy their legal obligations. However, these basic requirements do not guarantee success unless the ethos of the school is one that condemns bullying in all its forms and sends out unequivocal messages that such behaviour will not be tolerated and that perpetrators will be appropriately dealt with. The institutional structure of schools is one based on authority, status and power and those hierarchical divisions themselves can lead to abuses of power as can the *classification* of pupils based on their level of attainment or the nature of their needs.

Staff values and attitudes can have a significant impact on a school's success in reducing bullying. Staff members who believe that low level bullying is the norm and is an inevitable part of a young person's educational life are more likely to demonstrate bullying behaviours themselves. These may include overt ridiculing and humiliating of pupils for minor infringements or underperformance in lessons. Professional development for whole staff groups can help break down the stereotypical myths surrounding bullying. If staff contribute to the development of the Bullying Policy they are more likely to demonstrate ownership of, and commitment to, its underpinning values. An ethos of mutual respect between pupils and staff, supported by the setting out of key principles, can set the standards for pupil/staff interaction.

Awareness-raising on the part of all sections of the school community will help to promote a positive and protective ethos within the school. Pupil awareness can be raised through the formal subject-based curriculum and through the informal pastoral curriculum. Discussions between pupils, parents and governors can help to set consistent definitions and language that will help to identify bullying when it occurs. The increased media interest and reporting of bullying means that pupils and parents will be more prepared to talk openly about their feelings, and perhaps to a lesser extent, about their experiences.

On a practical level, schools should record incidents of bullying to identify where and when bullying occurs to enable strategies to be put in place to prevent its occurrence.

Bullying will often take place during loosely structured activities and during break and lunch periods when there is less supervision or where the supervisors are regarded as having less authority.

Whatever success is achieved by a school in combating bullying, the staff will be faced with a situation where an incident of bullying will require action. The pupil and their parents will understandably be expecting firm and positive action and perhaps there will be an expectation that the perpetrator is excluded from the school. Punishment will often be appropriate, but punishment alone may serve to create feelings of resentment on the part of the perpetrator and it may be all too easy to impose sanctions that in themselves may be seen as bullying or at best oppressive. Alongside the use of punishment, an assessment of the needs of the bully may be an effective way of understanding and addressing their behaviour in the longer term. A *no blame* approach can be helpful in condemning the bullying behaviours rather then the perpetrator.

Restorative measures, or *making amends* for the distress caused to the victim can help the perpetrator understand the impact of their behaviour whist empowering the victim by giving them the evidence that their distress has been acknowledged and addressed by both the school and the bully.

Peer mentoring, peer counselling and peer mediation are all methods that can contribute successfully to tackling bullying by addressing the covert nature of bullying which relies on the belief that the victim will be too frightened to approach a member of staff. *Telling teachers about bullying was associated with a wide range of risks, particularly in relation to possible breaches of confidentiality, failure to act on reported incidents of bullying, and an inability to protect pupils from retaliatory action on the part of the perpetrators* (*Oliver and Candappa*, 2003, p4).

Peer pressure is a powerful influence over the behaviour of individual pupils. Bullying *courts* and school councils can help to formalise *pupil power* and can be useful ways of providing pupils with the means to resolve their problems and to agree longer-term solutions.

The demands placed on school managers are heavy and diverse and an investment of staff resources and time in yet another initiative may prove to be too daunting and of a lower priority than one that will result in higher standards in the classroom and better results for the league tables. However, the effects of bullying can be destructive to the well-being and safety of a significant number of pupils and these effects in turn will affect pupil progress and achievement. Effective policy and practice to address bullying will pay dividends in both pupil performance and reduced pressure on staff to deal with the after effects of bullying.

Parenting contracts and parenting orders – Anti-social Behaviour Act 2003

A *parenting contract* may be used as a mechanism for securing parental co-operation and support in managing pupil behaviour. These are voluntary agreements between the school and the parents. There is no penalty for failure by the parent to comply nor is there any civil liability on the part of the school in the event of failure to fulfil agreed actions.

As noted in Chapter 3 in relation to school absence, *parenting orders* were introduced in 1999 as part of the Crime and Disorder Act 1998. They are given to parents of young people who offend, truant or who have received a child safety order, or sex offender order. They can last three months and can be extended to 12 months.

The LEA may also apply for a parenting order in respect of the parents of permanently excluded pupils. This will only be appropriate for the most serious behaviours such as excessive or persistent violence and assaults, extensive damage or arson.

Parents must attend counselling or guidance sessions. Failure to do so can be treated as a criminal offence and the parent can be prosecuted. (For intervention options, see Chapter 8.)

The concept of inclusive education

The idea of *School's In* does not, and should not, refer only to processes by which disaffected, absent, truanting or excluded young people can become *included*. If we add in children and young people who are different – by virtue of their disability, their special needs, their different abilities and capacities – then we can begin to talk about a genuinely inclusive education. The origins of the inclusive education movement lie in the progressive extension of the integration agenda during the 1980s, particularly in relation to children with disabilities. Alan Dyson (cited in Clough and Corbett, 2000, p85) pays tribute to Tony Booth's 1983 definition of special needs *as those needs to which schools currently do not respond* and suggests this to be the only definition that is needed. Elsewhere, Dyson notes the alignment of the concept of inclusive education with the wider concept of social inclusion, by stating that inclusive education is about *ensuring every part of the education system is aligned with inclusive values ... schools can only be inclusive within the context of an inclusive education system* (Dyson, 2002, p127).

An inclusive school has to be mindful of concepts of *cultural capital. Many students who are low-attainers or under-achievers and who live in adverse social circumstances bring with them resources that enable them to engage in only limited ways with school learning as traditionally understood* (Dyson, 2002, p133). According to Slavin (2001), such children need maximum support which takes the form of consistent and coherent teaching approaches, the creation of a stable and purposeful learning environment in the school, the enlistment of family and community support for learning and intervention in students' out-of-school problems where necessary. In summary a truly *inclusive* school has to be able to ... *apply well founded and coherent strategies to the relatively large numbers of children who are at risk of exclusion because of their limited social resources and to respond creatively to individuals who do not fit neatly into these large scale strategies and demand a more individualized response* (Dyson, 2002, p133).

So, how might we recognise an inclusive school? You might want to attempt the following activity when keeping in mind pupils with particular needs, or with specific behavioural difficulties.

Try to identify the characteristics of an inclusive school setting:

(1)

(2)

(3)

(4)

(5)

Comment

For Lisky and Gartner (1999, pp17–18), cited in Dyson (2002, p131), inclusive schools have the following key features:

- *school-wide approaches – philosophy accepted by all stakeholders;*
- *all children can learn – and all can benefit when the learning is done together;*
- *a sense of community – belongingness;*
- *services-based on individual need not category;*
- *natural proportions – students with special needs being equitably distributed across the school;*
- *support provided in general education;*
- *teacher collaboration;*
- *curriculum adaptation – enabling all to benefit from the common curriculum;*
- *enhanced instructional strategies;*
- *standards and outcomes.*

So, what are the key characteristics of the inclusive school?

According to Dyson (2002, p133): *... many students who are low-attainers or under-achievers and who live in adverse social circumstances bring with them resources that enable them to engage in only limited ways with school learning as traditionally under-stood. This is not, of course, to say that they do not bring other kinds of resources, but it does mean that they will learn school-related knowledge and skills more effectively when they are given maximum support to do so.*

C H A P T E R   S U M M A R Y

We have introduced the ideas of *inclusive education* and *the inclusive school* here as a vehicle for seeing issues and problems in structural terms. Whilst the Children Act 1989 rightly affirms the needs, wishes and feelings of the individual child as the paramount concern of practitioners, it is equally essential that the child's needs be seen within an holistic context. As we noted in Chapter 1, the segregation of all children with differences was accepted without critical comment until relatively recently (the 1960s), and so the concept of inclusive education introduces us to a discussion of possibilities, or potentialities, of challenging assumptions, limitations and underestimations. We will therefore look at special educational needs in more detail in Chapter 6.

FURTHER READING

Newburn, T and Shiner, M (2005) *Dealing with disaffection: Young people, mentoring and social inclusion*. Devon: Willan.

This book looks as the broad spectrum of disaffection behaviours – offending, detachment from education, truancy and school exclusions – and offers some practical responses for professional teams

Reid, K (2000) *Tackling truancy in schools: A practical manual for primary and secondary schools*. London: Routledge.

A comprehensive manual for schools, addressing issues of causation and offering potential responses to truancy and absence.

Chapter 6
Related issues and practice challenges

We should not forget, therefore, that a parent caring for a disabled child may also be facing other stresses which, to them, may be far more problematic than those associated with the disabled child.
Beresford (1994, p111)

A C H I E V I N G   A   S O C I A L   W O R K   D E G R E E

This chapter will help you meet the following National Occupational Standards:

Key Role 1: Prepare for and work with individuals, families, carers, groups and communities to assess their needs and circumstances:
- Prepare for social work contact and involvement.
- Work with individuals, families, carers, groups and communities to help them make informed decisions.
- Assess needs and options to recommend a course of action.

Key Role 2: Plan, carry out, review and evaluate social work practice, with individuals, families, carers, groups, communities and other professionals:
- Interact with individuals, families, carers, groups and communities to achieve change and development to improve life opportunities.
- Identify the need for a legal and procedural intervention.

Key Role 5: Manage and be accountable, with supervision and support, for your own social work practice within your organisation:
- Work within multi-disciplinary and multi-organisational teams, networks and systems.

It will also introduce you to the following academic standards as set out in the social work subject benchmark statement (Quality Assurance Agency for Higher Education (QAA), 2000):

3.1.5 The nature of social work practice
- The characteristics of practice in a range of community-based and organisational settings including group-care, within statutory, voluntary and private sectors, and the factors influencing changes in practice within these contexts.
- The nature and characteristics of skills associated with effective practice, both direct and indirect, with a range of service users and in a variety of settings including group-care.

Children with special needs – educational and other issues

According to the Department for Education and Skills (DfES) (2005b), around 770,000 (7 per cent) of children in the UK are currently defined as disabled, of which only 4 per cent are supported by the provision of social services. Importantly, the Government also estimates that 29 per cent of these children live in poverty.

Within the contemporary landscape, 251,000 pupils had statements of special educational needs (SENs) in January 2003, this being the equivalent to 3 per cent of the school population, and about 20 per cent of pupils will need extra help at some point in their school careers. Government statistics show that 18 per cent of primary school children have SENs, whilst the figure for secondary schools is 15 per cent (source: **www.dfes.gov.uk/trends/index**).

Significantly, 60 per cent of pupils with statements were placed in mainstream schools whilst those in pupil referral units or special schools amounts to 35 per cent. However, SEN pupils are under represented in the most successful schools (source: DfES, 2003b), and less than 50 per cent of schools have accessibility strategies and plans (as required under the Disability Discrimination Act 1995). (See Appendix 2 for a checklist for identifying barriers to access and inclusion.)

It is worth noting that 91 of the country's 1,148 special schools have closed or been amalgamated since 1997 and many disability rights campaigners wish to see this process accelerated. Campaign 2020 aims, as its name suggests, to get all special schools closed by 2020, and is most concerned by the apparent rethink, or *volte face*, by Mary Warnock and others about the viability of total inclusion.

ACTIVITY **6.1**

Before we proceed any further, it is instructive for you to acknowledge your own values and assumptions about this debate. The question worth considering is: do you think all special schools should be closed, in pursuit of universal inclusive education, or is there a significant enduring role for special education schools and units?

Please note down your thoughts:

Comment

Of course, there is no right answer to this question. Some disabled children, disabled adults, their families, carers and supporters are vociferous advocates for separate education. Those in the deaf community, in particular, argue for separate schools on the grounds that, like faith schools, they are meeting the needs of a defined and separate community, characterised by the common bond of an acknowledged language. For them, the orthodoxy of integrated education is tantamount to assimilation and oppression of a marginalised group.

In January 2005, 242,600 pupils in England had statements of SENs, of which 60 per cent were placed in maintained mainstream schools (a slight reduction from 60.3 per cent in 2003). There has been an increase of children with special needs being placed in pupil referral units. Furthermore, it is estimated that there are about 1,230,800 unstatemented pupils who have SENs.

Practices clearly vary significantly across the UK. One recent report (on patterns in England) shows that pupils with special needs in South Tyneside are 24 times more likely to be segregated than *equivalent* pupils in the London Borough of Newham (Centre for Studies on Inclusive Education, 2005). Of course, such statistics are crude indicators, and tell us nothing as to how well children are getting on, how happy (or otherwise) their parents, carers and other family members are with the provision, or how the education as on offer fits with broader, longer-term goals than those narrowly connected to statutory education.

The social work task

Social work with children with disabilities is often undertaken in specialist teams, albeit under the broad umbrella of children's services. Whilst disabled children have been historically subject to a medical model of disability and difference (see Shakespeare, 2000), the social work contribution has been to advocate for and promote a social model (alongside the medical and educational perspectives), which addresses the needs of the child and their social system (family and carers). As this book is essentially about the relationship between social work and education, then we will focus upon issues of special schooling, integrated education policies and social inclusion policies.

However, we will begin by looking at what disabled children and young people have to say about their hopes, aspirations and expectations.

Understanding the aspirations of disabled children

ACTIVITY 6.2

What do think disabled children say about what is important to them? Try to list four key things.

(1)

(2)

(3)

(4)

Comment

Hughes (2005, p75) cites the National Service Framework for Children, Standard 8, which states that young people want to:

- *be listened to when decisions are being made about their lives;*

- *have friends of the same age or share similar experiences;*

- *do the same things as other children and young people of their age – shopping, going to the cinema, clubbing, going to youth and sports clubs, playing football etc;*

- *have the opportunity to be involved in out-of-school activities;*

- *be safe from harassment and bullying.*

These aspirations all serve to support policies of integration, and link to ideas of *ordinary lives*. Hughes (2005, p79) also quotes from the National Service Framework for children Standard 8: *Children and young people who are disabled or who have complex health needs receive co-ordinated, high quality child and family-centred services which are based on assessed needs, which promote social inclusion and, where possible, which enable them and their families to live ordinary lives.*

Will these standards be met? The aspiration of *Every Child Matters* and the new structures are that closer working relationships between universal services, like schools, and specialist services, like social work, will mean that children with additional needs can be identified earlier and supported effectively.

Interagency and inter-professional support for disabled children/ for children with special needs

The modern children's services practitioner needs to be familiar with the roles and functions of other professional services, such as:

- child and adolescent mental health services (CAMHS);

- hearing and visual impairment support services;

- speech and language services;

- occupational therapy and physiotherapy services; and

- specialist education support services.

Furthermore, many children who end up outside of mainstream education, in need of specialist support services, are there by virtue of special needs that fall into the category of behavioural support. Such children and young people do not have a defined physical or cognitive/learning disability, but rather fall into the arena of behavioural difficulties, as we explored in relation to attention deficit and hyperactivity disorder (ADHD) in Chapter 4.

Elective home education, education otherwise and alternative provision

The number of children and young people who are *home educated* has always been relatively small, although numbers appear to have increased steadily in recent years. It is apparent that as mainstream schooling has become progressively regulated and the product increasingly standardised, then there has been a small but not insignificant growth in elective home education. The Campaign for Real Education (2005) states that between 12,000 and 21,000 children are being home educated whilst other estimates, such as by a Nottingham University study (84,000) and by the Otherwise Club (150,000) produce significantly higher figures. The fact is that whilst the Government knows how many children feature every ten years in the census, and how many are registered with schools between census, and knows how many between the ages of 5 and 16 have been registered with State schools, it does not know about the balance – are they in private education, are they temporarily overseas, or are they being home educated?

Available figures, as estimates, are politically charged, with the Government wishing to play up customer (parent) satisfaction with the education product, whilst the alternative education lobby seeks to highlight the *growth* of electively home educated children and young people. It is instructive, nevertheless, to reflect upon the possible motivations for such a significant choice.

ACTIVITY **6.3**

What do you think are the reasons most often given by parents/carers as to why they choose to home educate *their child/children? Try to note down four reasons:*

(1)

(2)

(3)

(4)

Comment

You might have noted some or all of the following explanations:

- poor standard of teaching;

- the child is subject to bullying/discrimination in school by other children;

- the child is subject to bullying/discrimination in school by staff;

- the child's particular/special needs are not being recognised or met;

- negative influence of other children;

- religious/moral/ethical objections to the curriculum;

- a political critique of State controlled education;

- a belief in *free* education as a learning philosophy.

Most available studies have identified three clusters of specific justifications and motivations by parents choosing home education.

(1) *Concerns about discipline and safety in schools*: This refers to children having been subject to teasing, taunting, bullying, verbal abuse and violence – with teachers being perceived as powerless (or unmotivated) to protect the children.

(2) *Curriculum and quality of instruction*: This arena of concern is focused on class sizes, the quality of teaching staff, the availability of resources and the nature of the increasingly imposed and standardised curriculum.

(3) *Religious and ideological dissent*: This final cluster brings together those concerned about the allegedly amoral culture in schools and the immoral or secular nature of learning, with libertarians committed to the concept of free education and resistance to State education as a form of indoctrination.

So, if parents or carers choose to pursue the goal of home education, for whatever reason, what is the legal situation? As noted in Chapter 3, section 7 of the Education Act 1996 states that the parent of a child who is of compulsory school age has a legal duty to cause him (or her) to receive efficient full-time education suitable: (a) to his/her age, ability and aptitude, and (b) to any special educational needs he/she may have, either by attendance at school or *otherwise*. The term *otherwise* provides parents and carers, subject to certain conditions, with the option of educating their children outside the mainstream school system. With the exception of children with a statement of SENs, parents do not in fact need the permission of the local education authority (LEA) to follow this course of action, nor do they need to inform the LEA. However, they are required to inform the school when it is their intention to remove a child from a school roll (if the child has been enrolled there).

The concept of *suitable education* has, not surprisingly, caused heated and lengthy debate and legal dispute. In the 1985 case of *R* v *Secretary of State for Education and Science ex parte Talmud Torah Machzikei Hadass School Trust*, Mr Justice Woolf held that: *education is 'suitable' if it primarily equips a child for a life within the community of which he is a member, rather than the way of life in the community as a whole, as long as it does not foreclose the child's options in later life to adopt some other form of life if he wishes to do so* (cited by Education Otherwise).

If a parent elects to educate their child at home, they are responsible for the provision of all materials and for all of the associated costs. However, many LEAs offer advice and support beyond that prescribed within their statutory responsibilities. Parents may, at any time, return their child to mainstream education.

The LEA has only limited powers and rights to assist it in undertaking the duty to assess and monitor the appropriateness of the education provided. That said, if the LEA is not satisfied that a child is receiving an appropriate education, it must serve a school attendance order on the parents. The order requires parents, within 15 school days, to enrol their child in a mainstream school or to provide evidence that the child is receiving an appropriate education. As we have already seen in Chapter 3, *if a parent on whom a school attendance order is served fails to comply with the requirements of the order, he is guilty of an offence, unless he proves that he is causing the child to receive suitable education otherwise than at school* (Education Act 1996 (section 443)).

(For further information on elective home education, see Appendix 3 for the contact details of relevant organisations.)

Child employment

As we noted in Chapter 1 (and in the timeline at Appendix 1), the removal of children from the workplace from the early nineteenth century onwards formed the basis by which the State began to legally define the concept of childhood, and progressively linked the prohibition on child employment to compulsory participation in education. In Chapter 5, we noted that protecting children and young people from involvement and exploitation in the labour market is a long standing and central part of the education welfare service portfolio of responsibilities. That said, the law does allow for children and young people to have some opportunities to engage in paid employment, with the most common example being children involved in various forms of performance and entertainment, such as theatre, circus, ballet, or singing. Various regulations govern these activities, and define how the child's education is to be assured concurrent with their performance schedule.

However, of greatest concern is the widespread practice of young people being engaged in often illegal and potentially dangerous employment at the expense of their education. In this sense, the policing of illegal child employment practices represents the height of child protection responsibility for the education welfare service.

There are clear and established links between child poverty and child labour, and thus the issues of employment is most likely to involve the sensitive regulation of socially excluded groups, such as economic migrant, asylum seeker and refugee communities.

By way of illustrating the tensions and difficulties confronting the practitioner, the following extended case study addresses these complexities, and invites you to devise an intervention action plan.

Regulating child employment

CASE STUDY

The education welfare service has received a telephone call from a concerned resident who says that a Portuguese family has been living in the house next door for the last four months. The father and his three sons are believed by the caller to be engaged by a gang master who supplies labour to local market gardeners. The caller believes that one of the sons, Jose, is about 14 years of age and asserts that he is not attending school. Details are taken and the education welfare officer (EWO) visits the family home to be told by the

▶

mother – who is only able to communicate in English in a limited manner – that Jose does not want to go to school as he is happy working with his father and brothers at a vegetable and fruit packaging company 15 miles away. She is unable to produce any documentation to show Jose's age, but is willing to let the EWO borrow a photograph of Jose.

The named packing company has caused previous concerns with the education welfare service by employing school age children and it is agreed that an EWO will visit the company premises to check its employment records. The EWO and her manager visit the company premises and are told by the supervisor that they no longer employ young people under the age of 16. A check of the company's register of casual labour shows that all the employees have national insurance numbers, but the supervisor, on being shown Jose's photograph, admits that he does employ Jose and is waiting for him to produce his papers. He agrees to terminate Jose's employment immediately. A written warning will be sent to the managing director of the company. As a consequence of this intervention, Jose's father rings the education welfare service office in an angry and agitated state, demanding to see the people responsible for getting his son the sack.

Subsequent action

A member of the education welfare service visits the family home with a Portuguese-speaking community worker, who can facilitate and promote communication between the parties. It is explained to Jose's father and mother that he cannot legally be employed and that should he be injured at work, then the employer's liability insurance would be invalid. The parents are advised that Jose must, by law, receive an education suitable to his age, ability and aptitude.

Jose is in fact 15 years of age and has limited English but he is able to convey, in no uncertain terms, that he has no intention of going to the local school. His father supports his son's stance but, after a discussion about Jose's interests and aptitudes, he and Jose do agree to the possibility of a vocational placement that includes *key skills* training.

The local education authority has arrangements with a range of local training providers who are able to offer placements to young people at Key Stage 4, but for whom mainstream school is inappropriate or inaccessible. All of these placement settings are registered with the local authority and are able to provide key skills tuition together with a range of vocational training programmes. Staff members have been the subjects of Criminal Records Bureau disclosure and the premises are subjected to regular monitoring visits.

Jose is referred to the placement panel that agrees he should be offered a training placement at a firm of agricultural engineers. An officer will visit the family to explain the nature of the placement and to make arrangements for Jose to spend a day at the placement to make sure it is appropriate.

A Portuguese community worker will support Jose during the early stages of his placement at an agricultural engineering company and Jose will be transported to the placement by taxi.

The placement is deemed to be a mode of *educational provision* within the provisions of the Education Act 1996. Jose's attendance at such a placement would therefore satisfy the legal requirement for him to receive education. However, his parents will be deemed to be guilty of an offence if Jose fails to attend the placement on a regular basis.

ACTIVITY **6.4**

What should be the actions of the EWO? Using your knowledge and understanding gained from the previous chapters, try to note down a 5-point action plan.

(1)

(2)

(3)

(4)

(5)

C H A P T E R S U M M A R Y

In this chapter we have looked at three distinct groups: firstly, children with disabilities who, in educational terms, become defined as children with special, or additional needs; secondly, children and young people who are home educated; and finally, young people whom are in employment.

We now move our attention to considering the needs of another group, who indeed merit a chapter of their own, namely, children looked after by the local authority, and will consider in particular their educational needs and achievements.

FURTHER READING

Hughes, J (2005) 'Specific Areas of Practice with Children and Families: Children with Disabilities' in M. Jowitt and S. O'Loughlin (eds) *Social work with children and families*. Exeter: Learning Matters.

TUC/MORI Poll (2001) *Half a Million Kids Working Illegally*, TUC Report, 21 March 2001.

Chapter 7
Educational outcomes and children looked after

It is through school that children earn passports to different kinds of futures.
(Sonia Jackson, 2001, p134)

It's a national shame that the state is such a bad parent.
(Baroness Morris, Chair of Children's Workforce Development Council)

Getting it right for looked after children is about improving service for all children –
because their experiences highlight how robust and inclusive policies and practices
really are for all children.
(Firth and Fletcher, 2001, p157)

A C H I E V I N G   A   S O C I A L   W O R K   D E G R E E

This chapter will help you meet the following National Occupational Standards:

Key Role 1: Prepare for and work with individuals, families, carers, groups and communities to assess their needs and circumstances:
- Prepare for social work contact and involvement.
- Work with individuals, families, carers, groups and communities to help them make informed decisions.
- Assess needs and options to recommend a course of action.

Key Role 2: Plan, carry out, review and evaluate social work practice, with individuals, families, carers, groups, communities and other professionals:
- Interact with individuals, families, carers, groups and communities to achieve change and development to improve life opportunities.
- Identify the need for a legal and procedural intervention.

It will also introduce you to the following academic standards as set out in the social work subject benchmark statement (Quality Assurance Agency for Higher Education (QAA), 2000):

3.1.5 The nature of social work practice
- The characteristics of practice in a range of community-based and organisational settings including group care, within statutory, voluntary and private sectors, and the factors influencing changes in practice within these contexts.
- The nature and characteristics of skills associated with effective practice, both direct and indirect, with a range of service users and in a variety of settings including group care.

Facts and figures

On 31 March 2004, there were 61,100 children looked after by local authorities in England, almost 11,700 in Scotland, 4,516 in Wales and 2,446 in Northern Ireland.

For the looked after children and young people, the Children Act 2004 introduces a new duty for local authorities to promote their educational welfare (although, regrettably, it does not place a similar duty upon schools). Why has this new duty been introduced?

As noted earlier, a recognition of the paucity of academic attainment amongst this group of young people has slowly emerged over the past 20 years – from the first studies of Jackson (1987), to the publication of *Patterns and Outcomes* by the Department of Health in 1991 and then to more recent data since the introduction of the Quality Protects programme in 1998, culminating in highly critical evidence from the Social Exclusion Unit study of 2003. To restate the point, note the following outcomes:

- Only 43 per cent of care leavers achieve at least one GCSE or GNVQ upon leaving care, compared with 95 per cent of the population as a whole (Department for Education and Skills (DfES), 2005).

- Only 6 per cent achieve the *benchmark* of five or more GCSE subjects at A*–C grade, as opposed to 53 per cent of all children, and over half leave school with no formal qualifications of any kind (DfES, 2005).

- In terms of progression outcomes, less than 1 in 100 children who leave care go onto higher education/university, compared with 43 per cent of young people who live with birth parents (National Children's Home (NCH), 2005).

Making sense of underachievement

ACTIVITY 7.1

Why do you think looked after children and young people have much lower attainment outcomes in terms of GCSEs and other such indicators? Try to identify at least 4 factors:

(1)

(2)

(3)

(4)

Comment

You might have identified such factors as:

- disrupted educational *careers* caused by frequent moves;
- exclusions – both fixed term and permanent;

- low expectations from teachers, social workers, parents, carers, and from the child her/himself;

- bullying, labelling and discrimination.

In fact, research on children *looked after* consistently identifies a number of longstanding and persistently present factors associated with extremely poor levels of school attainment:

- damaging pre-care experiences;

- non-attendance at school;

- emotional stress experienced prior to and during care;

- inadequate liaison between carers and schools;

- low expectations of carers and teachers;

- prioritisation of welfare above educational concerns;

- disruption caused by placement moves and the low priority given to education when moves are being arranged (Stein and Carey, 1986; Jackson, 1988, both cited in Newburn and Shiner, 2005, p9). (In fact research evidence has shown that if you minimise the number of placements (as targeted by the Quality Protects programme) then educational achievements improve significantly. This effect is particularly noticeable if a child or young person is in a stable foster care setting for 12 or more months.)

Furthermore, the Social Exclusion Unit's (SEU) report *A Better Education for Children in Care* (SEU, 2003) identified five key reasons why such children underachieve in education:

(1) their lives are characterised by instability;

(2) they spend too much time out of school;

(3) they do not have sufficient help with their education if they fall behind;

(4) primary carers are not expected or equipped to provide sufficient support and encouragement for learning and development; and

(5) they have unmet emotional, mental and physical health needs that impact on their education.

To refer to a final study, research by Francis (2000, p28) explored the following factors:

- the place of education within social workers' priorities in relation to looked after children;

- perceptions of the corporate parenting role;

- the expectations of social workers, carers and teachers in relation to children's educational performance.

In the study, none of the social workers identified education as a high priority. Few social workers visited their service users' schools (often leaving this task to carers) and teachers did not attend reviews. Teachers and social workers had low expectations, but this may be seen as a realistic consequence rather than as a cause, *per se*, of underachievement. It is worth emphasising that consistent findings from studies do not identify low ability, behaviour problems or learning needs as valid explanations for such stark underachievement, but a lack of adequate educational support for children looked after.

Since evidence all served to confirm and compound the views of Jackson (1994, p273) when she had referred to a *deep split between education and care which runs through all of our institutions and services for children*, it has been (reluctantly) acknowledged by many researchers that social workers, as a generalised professional group, have devalued the significance of education as an outcome for children and young people. Specific research by the Dartington Research Unit and Jackson (as summarised in *Patterns and Outcomes* (Department of Health, 1991)), all testified to the paucity of attention paid by social workers to the arena of education, to school attendance and achievement. Further research (Fletcher-Campbell, 1997; Jackson and Sachdev, 2001) reinforced the critical perspective. It was therefore not surprising that educational attainment for those within the looked after system became a key objective of the Government's Quality Protects programme (Department of Health, 1998a).

The Quality Protects objectives

This project emerged from the White Paper, *Modernising Social Services* (Department of Health, 1998b), and had the following key elements:

- new national objectives for children's services, which set out clear outcomes for children, and gave precise targets to be achieved in relation to educational qualifications;

- an important role for local councillors in exercising their duties as corporate parents of children in public care;

- an annual evaluation of a council's Quality Protects Management Action Plan;

- partnership within and between central and local government agencies and the health service in pursuit of *joined up* services.

The detailed target for education was to *improve the educational attainment of children looked after, by increasing to at least 50% by 2001 the proportion of children leaving care at 16 with a GCSE or GNVQ qualification and to 75% by 2003* (Department of Health, 1998b).

(Although subsequently modified, the existence of these targets attested to the Government's critical conviction that local authorities were failing as *corporate parents* to take seriously the educational achievements of children and young people in public care.)

In 2003, the SEU reported on a two-year study of the education of looked after children and young people. The findings were that, despite increased resources, change had been hampered by: workforce capacity issues; insufficient commitment at a management level; a lack or poor use of resources; a lack of joint working across disciplines and agencies and low expectations by professionals and the wider society (SEU, 2003). It is worth noting that a persistent legalistic anomaly in the system is that the local education authority cannot prosecute itself (its children's services wing) for failing to educate children in public care – even though it has corporate and collective responsibility for a child looked after.

Furthermore, the progressive *liberalisation* of local education authority control over the local management of schools – with schools acquiring autonomy in terms of admissions policy and process – has meant that the corporate parent (the local authority) finds it increasingly difficult to get schools to actually educate those particular children and young people with the most difficult and damaging histories, and for whom it has the most direct responsibility – in other words, children and young people in public care.

Another stream of critical literature has identified the failure on the part of social workers to recognise the value of educational institutions and agencies in terms of child abuse identification, investigation, and as general support systems to children, young people and their families, that promote resilience and security.

In a broader vein, Gilligan (1998, pp14–15) identifies numerous important roles for schools in relation to looked after children:

- school as ally;

- school as guarantor;

- school as capacity builder for children;

- school as secure base;

- school as integrator;

- school as gateway to opportunities in adulthood;

- school as a resource for parents and communities.

Before proceeding to look at the educational outcomes of looked after children, we will reflect upon the situation of one of the case studies set out in the Introduction.

CASE STUDY

Chantelle is a black British young woman, in Year 11, with just two terms to complete before her GCSE exams. She is a looked after young person, under section 20 of the Children Act 1989, and is resident in a foster home. Her school has been severely disrupted by frequent moves and changes over the past five years, but she is committed to taking her exams. Her personal education plan is being reviewed.

__Further information:__ Issued as joint guidance by the then Department for Education and Employment and the Department of Health in 2000, the Education of Young People in Care circular stated that all looked after children should be provided with a personal education plan (PEP) within 20 days of entering care or joining a new school. The PEP should set out the child's achievements, their needs and aspirations, and should ensure access to services and support. The assumption is that the PEP contributes to a stability of education and schooling, by identifying particular and special needs, by establishing clear goals and by recording progress and achievements.

ACTIVITY 7.2

Based upon your own experience of schooling, what key elements would you expect to see identified in Chantelle's PEP?

(1)

(2)

(3)

(4)

Comment

The range of education and development needs to be covered in a PEP should include:

- accessing nursery or other high quality early years provision where appropriate to the child's age (e.g. playgroups);

- on-going catch-up support for those who have fallen behind with school work;

- providing suitable education where a child is not in school, e.g. because of temporary or permanent exclusion;

- transition support needs and integration when children begin to attend a new school or return to school (e.g. following illness or exclusion);

- out-of-school hours' learning activities/study support and leisure interests;

- school attendance and, where appropriate, behaviour support;

- the necessary level of support to help the child to achieve well at each National Curriculum Key Stage, particularly in completing an appropriate range of approved qualifications;

- support needed to achieve long-term aspirations for further and higher education, training and employment.

Practical support for children looked after

Research by Martin and Jackson (2002) focused on *success*, and sought to identify the factors seen as most important by a group of *high achiever* young people in public care. These respondents highlighted some practical issues, such as access to and provision of:

- laptops/computers;

- revision guides;

- art materials;

- home tutors;

- transport to school/college;

- a quiet space to do homework;

- safe storage space.

Furthermore, another study of the experiences of high achievers identifies the following protective factors that *may* lead to later educational success for children in care:

- *stability and continuity in care arrangements;*

- *reading competence (learning to read early, and being a fluent reader);*

- *a parent or carer who values education and sees it as a means to do well in life;*

- *friends outside care who do well at school;*

- *out-of-school interests and hobbies (these help build social skills and contacts with adults and young people outside the care system);*

- *a significant adult who offers consistent encouragement and support and serves as a mentor and prospective role model; and*

- *attending school regularly.*

(From Lincolnshire County Council: Education Protects *(date of publication unknown))*

A research summary

Jackson *et al* (2003) conducted a five-year study of university students with public care backgrounds. The point, in a nutshell, was to identify how these young people had *made it* educationally, against the odds, and in contrast to their *in care* peers. This is included in the further reading section (see below). Their findings are echoed in the *success story* from the London Borough of Merton, which can boast an achievement rate of 35 per cent looked after young people attaining GCSEs at grades A–C, compared with the national average of 9 per cent. The answer, according to the education inclusion manager, is *a teacher with expectations, a social worker who is involved and a foster carer who values education* (cited by Valios, 2005), and the gold standard importance of placement stability as the precondition for schooling continuity.

To illustrate these points, we will consider another extended case study.

Looked after child

Winston, a 14-year-old young person of African Caribbean heritage, has been made the subject of an emergency protection order following a major family breakdown during which his father was remanded in custody and his mother left the family home, destination unknown. Winston has been placed with the only available foster family who live some 35 miles from his own home and from his previous school. (The agencies within the local authority now have the role of corporate parent, and are collectively responsible for providing the level of care that any natural parents would demonstrate for all aspects of the young person's life.)

Winston enjoys school and, though still in Year 9, has set his sights on becoming a graphic designer. Winston's foster parents and social worker are keen to sustain Winston's academic success and feel that it is crucial that Winston continues at his current school to ensure the continuity of his educational success and to provide at least one element of stability in Winston's life at this difficult time. (A corporate parent must aim for continuity and stability, should have high expectations and should listen to the young person.)

Action

A meeting is convened at Winston's school. In attendance are Winston, his foster parents, social worker, local education authority (LEA) education officer for looked after children, and the designated teacher for looked after children. (Schools are required to have a designated teacher for young people who are looked after in the school. This person has responsibility for ensuring that the needs of looked after pupils are met and for liaising with outside agencies, ensuring pupil level plans are kept up to date and for maintaining the register of looked after pupils. The LEA keeps a register of the names of the designated teachers in all the schools in its area.)

All parties agree that Winston should remain at his present school as it is intended that Winston will return to his family home as soon as circumstances will allow. (Had it been appropriate for Winston to change schools, the local authority would have a duty to find a school place within 20 school days.)

The designated teacher with responsibility for looked after children, who teaches Winston for PE, will meet with Winston on a weekly basis to ensure that he is coping with the changes in his current circumstances and to respond in a timely way to any areas of concern. (Winston may have elected to meet with another member of school staff had he so wished though the designated teacher would still retain overall responsibility for co-ordinating the school's programme of support for Winston.)

The local authority feels it would be impossible for Winston to get to school by public transport and it is agreed that the education department will arrange for a taxi to collect and return Winston to his foster home. The taxi allocated is already transporting two other pupils on a journey that requires a small detour to accommodate Winston.

CASE STUDY continued

Winston's social worker will liaise with the designated teacher for looked after children on a weekly basis to ensure that the school are kept up-to-date with the developments in Winston's family circumstances and to ensure that Winston's strong educational progress is sustained.

The agreed actions will be set out in a PEP, which must be drawn up within seven days. This will form part of Winston's care plan. The plan will be reviewed after 28 days in line with the review of the care plan and then again after three months and six months. The plans may be reviewed at any time in response to changing circumstances or at the request of the child.

The 'By Degrees' study project

This project has sought to identify the effective support system for those students who have been formerly looked after, and who have progressed into higher education. Commissioned by the Frank Buttle Trust, and conducted by the Thomas Coram Research Unit, it focused on the 1–5 per cent of young people formerly looked after who progress into higher education, as compared with 43 per cent of the general population (NCH, 2005).

The particular needs identified by research study include:

- Foster carers need specific training to support children and young people as they aspire to enter higher education.

- Universities/Colleges of Higher Education should run open days specifically for foster carers and others engaged in support of vulnerable young people, to address particular issues; such as:

  (a) when young people enter university, does their status change from being in foster care into being in supported lodgings; and

  (b) where are young people who are looked after meant to go during university vacation?

- Significantly, the study showed that only 10 per cent of those formerly looked after who entered higher education dropped out, compared with the national average of 14 per cent.

Looked after children protocols

Under pressure from government, schools have been obliged to sign up to looked after children protocols, with a DfEE/Department of Health Circular (2000, p13) stating:

Local councils have a duty to establish and maintain a protocol for sharing relevant information about care, placements and education, including mechanisms for how social services, LEAs and schools share information. In practice it will be individual social workers who will be expected to liaise with schools and carers and ensure that essential information can be shared so that education is prioritised. Social workers should be aware of the educational needs, progress and aspirations of children with whom they are working.

The learning gateway

This service is targeted at 16 and 17 year olds who are outside of education, training or employment (NEET). Certain high-risk groups are targeted by this strategic service:

- care leavers;

- young people who offend;

- young people who are excluded from school;

- young people with special educational needs, in particular those with emotional and behavioural difficulties or drug/alcohol dependency;

- young people from certain ethnic minorities;

- long-term non attendees at school;

- teenage parents;

- young people with low levels of school achievement or basic skills.

Social work responses

So, given this wealth of research evidence pointing to a cluster of core determinants that may facilitate educational achievement, how are social work practitioners to respond? Isobel Brodie (2001) offers a summary of possible social work responses to the educational needs of looked after children and young people, arising from her empirical study of exclusions in particular. According to her study, social workers and residential childcare workers assume various positions:

Quiescence	Where social workers see their role as subordinate to teachers in relation to the child's education
Salvage	A reactive, crisis driven response, often reacting to one exclusion or difficulty after another
Experts	When a children's establishment is viewed as an educational resource itself, or when a foster carer might be engaged as a home educator
Advocacy	The worker assumes a central role in the educational welfare of young people, and explores a range of options
Collaborative support	Partnership working between named co-ordinators in school and named lead workers from children's services

Figure 7.1 *Responses to the education needs of looked after children*

Whilst advocacy might be necessary at times, the preferred position would appear to be collaborative support, creating a home-school partnership between the school and the local authority children's services.

C H A P T E R   S U M M A R Y

In summary, *school matters*, not only in terms of the impact of educational achievement for future prospects, but also in terms of itself, as a locale of vital and supportive relationships. Within a context of uncertainty – changing and unpredictable family relationships or often unstable foster care settings – *education is the aspect of children's lives where it is most essential to preserve continuity, in relationships with teachers and friends, attendance at lessons, keeping up with curriculum content, and ensuring understanding of important elements of each subject* (Jackson, 2002, p46).

As a final comment, it is worth noting that the Government is committed to expanding the State boarding school sector by about 1,000 places by the end of 2006. If boarding schools seem to be the *schooling of choice* for those with the most economic and social capital, when purchasing education in the private sector for their offspring, then might it be a solution for the most vulnerable children and young people – namely, those in public care? There are 34 State boarding schools in England and 1 in Wales. The DfES has confirmed it was *exploring the scope for making more use of boarding school provision for looked after children who have been excluded from mainstream education* (quoted in *Children Now*, 28/9 4 October 2005, p5). We will see what emerges from such a review.

FURTHER READING

Blyth, E and Milner, J (1997) *Social work with children: The educational perspective*. Harlow: Longman.

An older text, but introducing the reader to the range of social work activities connected to education.

Brodie, I (2001) *Children's homes and school exclusion*. London: Jessica Kingsley.

An important book, looking at the specific issues of children and young people who are looked after, and their vulnerability to school exclusion.

Chase, E, Simon, A and Jackson, S (eds) (2006) *In care and after: A positive perspective*. Abingdon: Routledge.

An up-to-date text, summarising the latest research concerning children and young people's experiences of being looked after.

Commission for Social Care Inspection (2005) *Making Every Child Matter: Messages from Inspections of Children's Social Services*. London: The Stationery Office.

Social Exclusion Unit (2003) *A Better Education for Children in Care*. London: Social Exclusion Unit/ Office of the Deputy Prime Minister.

Chapter 8

What are we going to do about it? Assessment and intervention

Il faut être enthousiaste de son métier pour y exceller
(To excel in one's chosen profession one must be an enthusiast).
(Diderot)

Anyone working with young people should advocate for them, agitate for change and endeavour to ensure that relevant strategies are implemented.
(Ann Wheal, 2004, p90)

A C H I E V I N G   A   S O C I A L   W O R K   D E G R E E

This chapter will help you meet the following National Occupational Standards:

Key Role 2: Plan, carry out, review and evaluate social work practice, with individuals, families, carers, groups, communities and other professionals:
- Interact to achieve change and development and to improve life opportunities.
- Address behaviour which presents a risk.

Key Role 3: Support individuals to represent their needs, views and circumstances:
- Advocate with and on behalf of individuals, families, carers, groups and communities.

Key Role 4: Manage risk to individuals, families, carers, groups, communities, self and colleagues:
- Assess and manage risks to individuals, families, carers, groups and communities.

Key Role 5: Manage and be accountable, with supervision and support, for your own social work practice within your organisation:
- Work within multi-disciplinary and multi-organisational teams, networks and systems.

It will also introduce you to the following academic standards as set out in the social work subject benchmark statement:

3.1.2 The service delivery context
- The issues and trends in modern public and social policy and their relationship to contemporary practice and service delivery in social work.
- The significance of legislative and legal frameworks and service delivery standards (including the nature of legal authority, the application of legislation in practice, statutory accountability and tensions between statute, policy and practice).

The illusion of objectivity

Whatever the mode of human services intervention with children, young people and their families or carers, it is explicitly or implicitly based upon an assessment, or a judgement about the person's circumstances, needs and requirements. However, it has to be recognised that assessment takes place within the context of the values of both the assessor and the assessed, the practitioner and the service user, although the structural, institutional and personal power of the assessor would generally indicate the paramountcy of her or his values within the assessment process.

Assessment is basically about making sense of a situation, by gathering information. According to Brown (1996, p22), *assessment is a necessary stage in defining what method of intervention would be most effective*, yet this activity always takes place within the context of the worker's own values and assumptions. As Payne (1991, p194) notes: *Workers will always be prejudiced by their own view of the world, and an examination of this prejudice should always be included in any assessment.*

Assessment as a theory driven activity

ACTIVITY *8.1*

Based upon your experience of social work, education or social care practice, what are the core components or stages of assessment as an activity?

Comment

To Thomas and Pierson (1995) an assessment contains at least four elements:

> (1) *Description – the person's characteristics, circumstances, family structure.*
>
> (2) *Explanation – suggesting possible causes and probable consequences.*
>
> (3) *Identification – problems to be resolved, strengths and weaknesses.*
>
> (4) *Evaluation – how a person's needs might be effectively met.*

Element (2) (*Explanation*) indicates the centrality of the assessor being aware of her/his own theoretical stance. Whenever a phenomenon of any description is subject to our processes of explanation, we are engaged in making sense of something, based upon our *ways of seeing* (Berger, 1972). This is, necessarily, a socially constructed process, which is complex and our conclusions are potentially contested, in that equal valid alternative theories can be proposed. Indeed, according to Clifford (1998, p233, cited in Parker and Bradley, 2003, p4): *... assessment has to partake of scientific, theoretical, artistic, ethical and practical elements ... something which has long been recognised by practitioners, and regarded as traditional in social work and all the helping professions.*

We will try to illustrate the complexity of assessment by thinking about a core issue that consistently affects the daily working of those engaged in education social work/education welfare practice. We will use one of the case studies first outlined in the Introduction. We will begin by offering very little information, to make the point that we can immediately begin to make sense of a situation – based upon our hypotheses, our past experience, our values.

CASE STUDY

Adam is a 10-year-old white child. He lives with his three brothers and his biological parents, who are both heroin users. Apart from his sporadic school attendance, there are significant concerns about his poor social skills, his chaotic behaviour, his risk of offending and his general safety.

ACTIVITY 8.2

As an education welfare officer, you have received this referral from the school. How do you make sense of this situation? What do you want to know? What is going to be the focus of your assessment?

Comment

You will probably have noted a number of things about Adam's situation:

- he is 10, and has three brothers;

- both of his parents are engaged in substance misuse behaviours; and

- he himself is beginning to develop problematic and concerning behaviours apart from absence from school.

You might have then suggested a number of linked hypotheses, such as:

- the substance misuse of the parents might mean the family live in relative poverty; and

- their substance misuse might mean they are periodically unable to care effectively for Adam and his brothers; so

- Adam is losing his childhood, by having to care for any of his brothers who might be younger than him, or who might have special needs, and which could explain his absence from school; and therefore

- he rebels against this pressure by getting into *bad company*, exposing him to various forms of risk, which might be based upon the problematic behaviour of his siblings or peers; and

- he is in danger of being *lost* to education before he has even completed the primary stage.

This represents a set of assumptions that forms a working model, a hypothesis, something to test out. Of course, all of these assumptions could be wrong. We will return to this case, once we have looked at assessment principles.

Principles of assessment: A checklist

Before proceeding with the case of Adam and his family, let us consider the principles that underpin ethical and effective assessment practices.

ACTIVITY 8.3

Using your experience of simple, core or complex assessments in any human services setting, try to identify the principles that balance the need of an organisation and its representative to assess a situation, and the rights of the person being assessed. List your thoughts below:

Comment

We are sure your thoughts reflected the importance of assessment as being of service user's gateway to accessing a service, or, in the case of statutory interventions, carry particular weight in terms of the judgements being made regarding the user's mental health, or parenting capacity, or suitability for a particular school, or response to an intervention programme that has already been offered.

We would therefore propose that in terms of working in children's services and education settings, the practitioner should endeavour to ensure that:

- Every assessment should be individually negotiated with service users (bad assessment diminishes the user and any vestiges of power held by her/him).

- The assessment should take place in a setting that maximises the power of the service user (procedural, clinical, office-based practice sets up barriers and only serves to emphasise the power of the assessor in comparison with the service user).

- All efforts should be made to ensure that the user understands the process, the timescale, the possible outcomes and what authority and power the practitioner holds.

- Anti-oppressive practices should inform and drive the assessment process, by avoiding the use of jargon, of inappropriate language, of acronyms, of shorthand, of oppressive language in general.

- The service user should understand who will read the written assessment document, its status, its shelf-life, where it will be stored, and be made aware of complaints procedures and of access to files entitlements and freedom of information rules.

- The assessment process has to attain that magical, creative, elusive balance between underplaying its importance (used to put the service user at ease), and overplaying its importance (by being honest about authority, and the uses to which the assessment might be put, but which might stifle expression and involvement).

- The practitioner needs to be sceptical of simple users' guides to assessments. They might be comforting, but are equally reductionist and mechanistic, and can be little more than a collection of *tick box* options.

- The practitioner should pay attention to *gut instincts* – practice experience counts for a lot, and feelings or hunches should be tested out, to seek evidence that may confirm or negate these instincts.

- The experienced practitioner is aware of the inevitable tendency to develop *scripts* – usually asking the same questions, in the same order. You might feel *If it works, don't fix it!*, but then again, you might learn from reflecting upon your developed *modus operandi*, and avoid the dangerousness that stems from being stale and non-reflective.

So, in terms of Adam, we will ultimately need, as integrated children's services, to make some judgement as to the parenting capacity of the adults to meet his needs and that of his brothers. Within the context of the *Framework for the Assessment of Children in Need and their Families* (Department of Health/Department for Education and Skills/Home Office, 2000), Calder and Hackett (2003, p160) have devised a variation that offers an integrative framework for the assessment of parenting capacity. Their model references to various research studies, which look at the inter-relationship between the three domains of *parental characteristics, the context of stress and support, and child characteristics*.

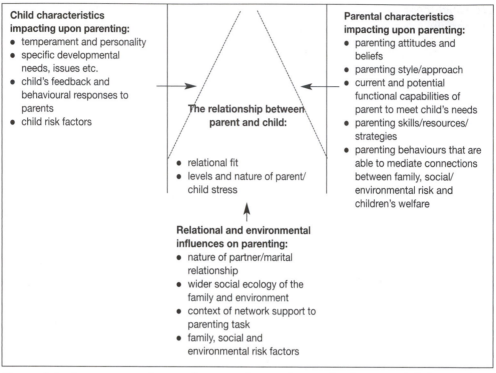

Figure 8.1 *Assessments of parenting capacity: An integrative framework (adapted from Calder and Hackett, 2003, p160)*

The research evidence appears to suggest that if all three domains were intact, then there would be positive outcomes for children. If *one* domain was weak, it could be offset, or buffered, by the other two. Thus the task of parenting a child with complex special needs could be carried out satisfactorily if parenting capabilities are high *and* support systems are in place and are effective. Similarly, parents with reduced capacity, perhaps due to unresolved issues from their own childhood, may nevertheless cope if the situation is offset by child and environmental factors that are positive. However, if *two or more* domains are weak, then this is a strong predictor of poor outcomes for children.

So, let us return to the case of Adam and his family. In order to further explore your responses to this scenario, we have provided further contextual information.

Adam is 10 years old. He is perceived as being out of control and to be displaying behavioural problems. He has recently received a police warning for taking a motor car without consent. He has a history of poor school attendance and his first referral to the education welfare service dates from when he was in nursery.

He is described as a very angry child who requires a lot of support in school due to the risk he can pose to other children. Adam shows no interest in school and he finds it difficult to sit and listen in class. He is a little better in one-to-one situations, but classroom settings, play and meal times are all risk events, when Adam requires intensive monitoring and supervision for his own safety and of others.

Adam is one of four male children. He and his younger brother (Ben) are the sons of Steven and Carol, whilst the two older brothers (Chris and Daniel) have a different father. Carol and Steven are both long-term drug users and when Adam and his brother were born, they were both experiencing the effects of drug withdrawal.

Over the years, all of the boys have experienced a lack of consistent parenting and have been exposed to risk behaviours within the home.

The education welfare service was actively involved from 2001, and a joint referral was made to social services by the education welfare officer and school staff in relation to Ben (the youngest child) who appeared to be in danger due to neglect and Carol's incapacity to care and protect him.

At the subsequent child protection case conference, all of the boys were placed on the Child Protection Register in 2001 (and the youngest three remain on the register).

Due to persistent poor attendance records, court convictions of the parents occurred in 2001, 2004 and 2005 for non-school attendance. The social services department (now children's services) initiated care proceedings in relation to the children, and a foster care setting was arranged. However, at the eleventh hour, Carol's mother and father (the boys' maternal grandparents) offered to accommodate the children – a development that coincided with Steven being sent to prison for theft. In fact, Carol and her children moved in with her parents. During this time, the boys attended school regularly and made some improvements in their social and educational development.

However, upon Steven's release from prison, Carol and the boys returned to live with him, with an associated decline in school attendance and the emergence of other difficulties.

Adam has been accused of robbing another child of a mobile phone and there is evidence of cruelty to animals – both concerns now being addressed by the youth offending team and an educational psychologist.

Adam's parents have also requested that he move schools – even though his current school is best placed to address his particular needs.

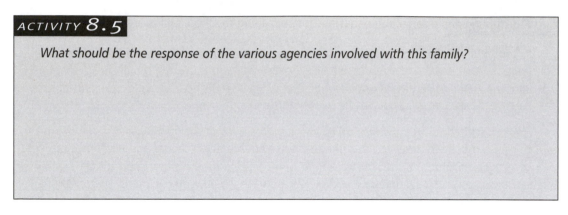

Comment

Multi-disciplinary or inter-professional practice needs to acknowledge that, due to differing organisational and policy objectives, different issues are at the forefront of their respective agendas.

(1) The schools have their own concerns about performance and attainment, and none of these children are likely to enhance their figures. In other words, admitting the children would represent a high risk/low gain action.

(2) The education welfare service is primarily concerned about securing regular and sustainable attendance. This might be achieved by getting the children admitted to a school favoured by the parents, or it might have no effect. The alternative strategy is to pursue further prosecutions against the parents.

(3) The social worker's focus has to be the safety and welfare of Adam and his brothers, and school attendance may not be seen as the most pressing issue, given the range of potential risks within this household.

Outcomes

A decision was taken to pursue care order proceedings with respect to the four boys, given the absence of any discernable improvement over the years, and the fact that the children were becoming disengaged at progressively younger ages. Whilst still at primary school, Adam is causing concern for schoolteachers, the educational psychologist, the police and youth offending team workers, and children's services.

Modes of intervention – achieving change

The focus of this book has been to try to understand and make sense of various types of problematic behaviour and situations, which merit the particular attention of education and social work services. These are:

- educational underachievement behaviours;
- truancy and non-school attendance behaviours;

- disrupting and disaffection behaviour (often leading to school exclusion);

- offending behaviour.

Whatever our role – as a practitioner engaged with children, young people and their families or carers – the undeniable fact remains that we are expected to do something, to intervene, to make something happen in short, to *achieve change*.

So how is change to be achieved? Before we answer this question, let us first of all set out some principles that have been adopted by an international body as the basis of all work with young people.

Principles of working with young people

The FICE (Federation Internationale des Communicatives Educatives) has developed a code of ethics for all of those working with young people, as follows:

> - *Value and respect a young person as an individual in their own right, in their role as a member of their family and in their role as a member of the community in which they live.*
>
> - *Respect the relationship of the young person to their parents, their siblings and other members of their family, taking account of their natural ties and independent rights and responsibilities.*
>
> - *Enable the normal growth and development of each individual young person to achieve their potential in all aspects of functioning.*
>
> - *Help each young person for whom they bear responsibility: by preventing problems where possible, by offering protection where necessary, by providing care and rehabilitation to counteract or resolve problems faced.*
>
> - *Use information appropriately, respecting the privacy of young people, maintaining confidentiality where necessary and avoiding the misuse of personal information.*
>
> - *Oppose at all times any form of discrimination, oppression or exploitation of young people and preserve their rights.*
>
> - *Maintain personal and professional integrity, develop skills and knowledge in order to work with competence, work co-operatively with colleagues, monitor the quality of services, and contribute to the development of the service and of policy and thinking in the field.*
>
> *(Cited in Wheal, 2004, p3)*

In terms of application of these principles, let us consider one of the case studies, and begin to think about how to achieve change.

CASE STUDY

Jim is a 15-year-old, Year 11 pupil. He has attended very little at school over the past few months, and is often not to be found at home. He sleeps at various locations around the town and mixes with older young people. He is known to be using various substances, such as heroin and amphetamines. He has funded his habit by stealing – from strangers and from the homes of his relatives.

ACTIVITY **8.6**

Try to answer the following questions and list down your ideas:

- *What is Jim getting out of the current set of circumstances?*

- *What might be the disadvantages?*

- *What might be his motivation to change?*

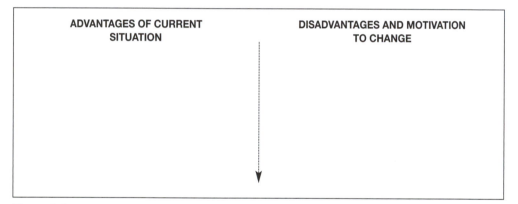

ADVANTAGES OF CURRENT SITUATION	DISADVANTAGES AND MOTIVATION TO CHANGE

Figure 8.2

Comment

In terms of advantages and benefits for Jim (the left hand column in Figure 8.2), you might have noted some or all of the following:

- excitement;

- belonging to a group;

- having a set of (older) mates;

- status and belonging;

- the *pleasures* of taking drugs;

- avoidance of school;

- the buzz of living from day-to-day;

- routine and ritual.

As for the disadvantages (the right hand column in Figure 8.2), your list might be shorter. We can however take an adult view, and be concerned about the following:

- his health;

- the short and long-term risks of infection or overdose;

- school failure and underachievement;

- about being 15 years old and having few prospects.

But these are essentially adult perspectives and concerns. So what might be Jim's sense of disadvantages and his motivation to change?

The anatomy of change

We need to acknowledge that there is a cycle of change, which has some key elements. Some practitioners find two aphorisms particularly helpful when thinking about bringing about change:

- *there is no gain without pain*, and

- *there is no change without loss.*

Such thoughts acknowledge that change is difficult, and that something has to be given up in order for new behaviours to replace them.

Working with the individual

(1) Life coaching and self coaching – using cognitive behavioural techniques

It is helpful when working with young people to identify *triggers*: events that trigger problem behaviours, such as missing school. Such discourse can lead onto *insight into high risk situations* – an awareness of when problem situations are about to occur, resulting in the development of *relapse prevention strategies*, based upon acquiring the skill of *positive self-talk*. Thus the focus of the intervention would be trying to work with the young person to identify the sequence that leads to either school absence or problematic behaviour within the school, that leads to disaffection and a risk of exclusion.

(2) The interviewing toolkit

The following key elements of interviewing would appear to help in the quest for change:

- good communication, including attentive and active listening, based upon *best practice* aspects of utilising counselling skills;

- a clear statement of boundaries and honesty about the worker's mandate and legal duties and the limits of confidentiality;

- working to specific aims and objectives with agreement as to the definition of progress and desired change;

- pro-social modelling of the values of respect, politeness and courtesy.

(3) Motivational interviewing

With its roots in work with people with addictions or substance misuse issues, this model is *based upon the concept that change is not an event but a cyclical process* (Cherry, 2005, p73), often requiring a progression through several stages until the desired change is achieved, and (more importantly) maintained and sustained. In terms of smoking cessation, for example, this translates into such slogans as *Never give up on giving up*. Ultimately, motivational interviewing is a therapeutic counselling technique that seeks to motivate change through negotiation rather than conflict. The optimistic and positive expectations of workers are a key determinant of change, and it is essential to evaluate practitioner attitudes from the outset. A study that Wilsher (1999) carried out with older children with special needs indicated that when staff gave children more choice and asked their opinions, the results demonstrated the extent to which they (the staff) had very often underestimated their pupils' abilities.

Essentially, motivational interviewing is about promoting and developing the inner resources of the service user – in this case, the child, young person and her or his family network. The key to change, as one might expect, is motivation, and Miller and Rollnick (2002, p10) sums this up in the phrase *ready, willing and able*. In other words, the service user understands the importance of change, has confidence in their ability to effect that change, and sees it as priority – in essence, the timing is right.

(4) Pro-social modelling

According to Cherry (2005, p3) *in every interaction with clients, practitioners have the opportunity to act as positive role models and to demonstrate formally and informally the behaviours and attitudes that are encouraging in those clients*. The key elements of practice include developing empathic relationships, exploring the legitimate use of authority, assertive interactions and pro-social feedback, motivating change and applying a systematic, collaborative, pro-social approach to problem solving. As Cherry (2005, p19) further notes, when applying pro-social modelling theory to school situations:

Positive behaviour management strategies and anti-bullying policies are underpinned by pro-social principles such as being clear what the rules are and implementing them quickly when necessary and expecting older children to act as role models for younger children.

We can conceptualise the behaviour of anyone in terms of its position between the tensions of immature or mature thinking, as set out below:

Table 8.1

Immature thinking	Mature thinking
Egocentric: thinking about yourself and not others	Sociocentric: actions are guided by thought about the consequences
Externally controlled: behaviour is determined by external sanctions	Internally controlled: behaviour is determined by an awareness of impact and consequences, and an internal dialogue
Concrete: seeing situations without reference to general principles, such as justice or impact on others	Empathic: ability to see things from the point of view of others

Table 8.1 *continued*

Instrumental: behaviour driven by short-term outcome	Pro-social: valuing personal relationships for their intrinsic – not instrumental – value
Impulsive: acting on the spur of the moment	Measured: thinking through actions
Short term: no awareness of longer-term consequences	Longer term: awareness of longer-term consequences of any action

Source: (Adapted from Lunness, 2000, as cited in Cherry, 2005, p12)

Because the concerns about school-based behaviour or absence relate to *minors*, then any intervention has to involve families, parents and carers. The following brief section looks at ways of working within the family system.

Working with the family

(1) Parental empowerment

To many practitioners engaged in a range of human services activities with children, young people and their parents or carers, the roots of a child's anti-social, criminal or problematic behaviour lies in the boundaries, or lack of them, within the home. According to John Dorkings (parent support worker with East Sussex Crime Reduction Initiatives): *Parents feel unable to set boundaries and we know children like them even though they kick against them ... they have almost lost control of the house and we tell them to go back and gain control, set house rules* (cited in *Community Care*, 2–8 February 2006)

In a scheme for those subject to parenting orders, practitioners enable parents to look at how the house is run – who does the washing up, how the clothes washing cycle is managed – which enables parents themselves to identify trigger points of conflict and determine priorities for the purpose of establishing rules and boundaries. Work on boundary setting is also accompanied by relaxation techniques and strategies for defusing conflict.

Furthermore, the techniques outlined above, regarding motivational interviewing and pro-social modelling, apply equally to work with parents and carers.

(2) Family group conferences

Based upon the belief that families can, with support, find their own solutions to the difficulties they are facing, this model of working evolved in New Zealand and is strongly influenced by Maori culture. The conference is not a single event, but is part of a process that requires clear information being shared with service users and transparent communication systems. At its simplest, it is a device for bringing together the minimum sufficient network in the kinship group to address a particular problem, and the conference group works through the four stages of:

(1) information giving – professionals set out concerns and issues and state the statutory, non-negotiable position (e.g. the child has to be educated);

(2) private planning time – the professionals leave and the *family* discuss the situation and devise a family plan to address the *problem*;

(3) agreeing the plan – the family invite professionals back in, and present their strategy;

(4) if the plan is adopted, then all present agree a process for monitoring and review.

(3) Solution-focused brief therapy

Solution-focused practice is a way of working that builds on the strengths of children, young people and families. This contributes to empowerment and the possibility of service users managing without the use of services over and above universal services. It also assists engagement and communication between practitioners and families.
(*Every Child Matters* (Green Paper))

The basis of the model is to acknowledge that most families can do lots of things well. They have often overcome lots of challenges, threats and difficulties, but then become stuck, or powerless, in the face of a particular problem – such as school attendance problems.

So, the trick is to try to harness their usual problem-solving mechanisms, usually through the use of a miracle question:

Suppose you go home, you do what you do this evening and then at some point you go to bed and go to sleep. And suppose that while you are asleep a miracle happens and the problems that brought you here are resolved. But since you are asleep you do not know that the miracle has happened. When you wake up tomorrow how will you find out? What will you notice that will say to you 'goodness, life is different – a miracle must have happened while I was asleep?'.

The question is asking the service user to identify the desired-for change, and to acknowledge that they cannot have both the problem and the solution – they have to have one or the other. Solution-focused brief therapy often follows the following sequence:

Table 8.2

Stage 1	Statement of the problem
Stage 2	Assess client(s) motivation
Stage 3	Develop solution orientation
Stage 4	Establish goals
Stage 5	Provide feedback and prescribe tasks

As with the pro-social modelling techniques, there is important behaviour to be evidenced by the school towards families. The use of persistent outreach efforts by the school team, such as letters and home visits, demonstrate to the child and his/her parents how much they matter to the school.

It is essential to determine *what works* – when are children attending without any difficulty, when are parents able to exercise parental control – and harness this dynamic. The key phrase here is *nothing succeeds like success* – an aphorism that applies equally to families, parents, carers, children, young people, organizational systems and practitioners.

CHAPTER SUMMARY

We have identified just a few of the techniques that are valuable components of the practitioner's *toolkit*, when trying to address the persistent issues of disaffection, disengagement, disruption, exclusion and absence, all of which become linked, in varying degrees, to risk behaviours such as offending, drug and alcohol misuse, sexual vulnerability and the consequences of such activities for current and future social exclusion.

A lot is to be gained by intervening successfully, and in Chapter 9 we will examine *what works*.

FURTHER READING

Beckett, C (2006) *Essential theory for social work practice*. London: Sage.

This new text contains useful sections on social work assessment and practice theory.

Cherry, S (2005) *Transforming behaviour: pro-social modelling in practice*. Cullompton: Willan Publishing.

A really comprehensive and practical summary of intervention techniques and models of practice.

Parker, J and Bradley, G (2003) Social work practice: *Assessment, planning, intervention and review*. Exeter: Learning Matters.

A helpful guide to undertaking assessments and the range of interventions that is available to the practitioner.

Chapter 9

What works?
The evidence base for
effective inclusive
education strategies

I and the public know
What all schoolchildren learn,
Those to whom evil is done
Do evil in return
(W. H. Auden, 1 September 1939 (1940))

In England an avowed commitment to inclusive education sits alongside legislation that
protects the existence of special schools, permits the exclusion of students for
disciplinary reasons and encourages a system of 'parental choice' that seems grossly
inequitable in its operation.
(Dyson, 2002, p138)

ACHIEVING A SOCIAL WORK DEGREE

This chapter will help you meet the following National Occupational Standards:
Key Role 6: Demonstrate professional competence in social work practice:
● Research, analyse, evaluate and use current knowledge of best social work practice.
● Contribute to the promotion of best social work practice.
It will also introduce you to the following academic standards as set out in the social work subject benchmark statement (Quality Assurance Agency for Higher Education (QAA), 2000):
3.1.4 Social work theory
● Research-based concepts and critical explanations from social work theory base of social work.

Introduction

Auden's statement above promulgates a belief that seems central to the thinking of many engaged in children's services, namely that children and young people who suffer abuse, rejection and neglect at school will, in turn, perpetrate abuse and violence on others. The days of institutional corporal punishment are, of course, long gone. Nevertheless, the impact of schooling – whether positive or negative – remains equally as powerful. We have shown earlier on in this book that there appears to be a significant correlation between school *failure*, at an individual level, and subsequent diminished opportunities with associated difficulties. So, how can this be altered? In this penultimate chapter, we will summarise and review recent research studies concerning the operation of policies and practices designed to maximise the opportunities of all children and young people within the education system.

Is anything working?

According to the National Audit Office (2005) government initiatives to cut truancy levels have amounted to the spending of £900 million, but with negligible effect. Between 1998 and 2004, the level of unauthorised absence has remained fairly steady at 0.7 per cent and the National Audit Office report *Improving School Attendance in England (2005)* suggested that: *There has been no decline in unauthorised absence, the causes of which have proved difficult to tackle.* These findings have been reiterated by the House of Commons Public Accounts Committee, which suggested that £885 million had been spent over seven years in trying to reduce the level of truancy, but with minimal gains (the *Guardian*, 2006). In fact, the Committee goes so far as to suggest that the number of children missing lessons each day, rather than falling, had risen by 5,000 in 2005.

Overall figures are disputed, and there clearly have been some gains in terms of attendance levels, but these are probably attributable to the reduction in formerly authorised absence, with fewer days being lost through holidays being taken during term time.

Nevertheless, and as explored in Chapter 4, the *tough* approach on absence has also coincided with an increase of 6 per cent in the number of exclusions – during 2003–04 a total of 9,980 children were permanently excluded and nearly 350,000 were excluded for fixed terms.

So, is anything really working?

Firstly, there is emerging evidence of real improvements in educational outcomes for many children and young people formerly in the looked after system. Much of this can be attributed to the impact of the Quality Protects initiative, the implementation of the Children (Leaving Care) Act in 2000, and the appointment of designated teachers in each school to work with social workers towards the goals identified in each child's personal education plan (PEP). Recent research (see Chase *et al*, 2006) is beginning to suggest that in fact children in public care are beginning to out perform vulnerable and disadvantaged young people outside the looked after system.

This last point is particularly pertinent. The long overdue level of attention paid to looked after children and young people shows that support, encouragement and advocacy all contribute to supporting pupils through difficult times and will achieve results. For many poor and disadvantaged young people outside of the looked after system, no such specialist and dedicated support systems exist.

However, education welfare services are attempting to build the capacity of schools to manage attendance and absence effectively. Much of this work depends upon social workers and education welfare practitioners helping schools to *open up* and involve parents in their children's learning (Whalley, 2001). Such approaches are supported by government evidence, which suggests that: *Parental involvement in education seems to be a more important influence than poverty, school environment and the influence of peers* (*Every Child Matters*, Green Paper, 1.12).

However, such statements run the risk of downplaying the importance of poverty, deprivation, alienation and other interconnected factors generally associated with social exclusion. Nevertheless, rather than blaming parents for the educational underachievement of their children, it is self-evident that the development and advancement of schools as places where adults can become involved, active and engaged can only result in positive outcomes all round. In order to achieve this, school staff groups (receptionists, support staff, teachers, headteachers) will all need to demonstrate the best aspects of pro-social modelling (as outlined in Chapter 8) in their dealings with parents, carers and communities. The Research into Practice group, in its response to the Green Paper, *Every Child Matters* suggested that the Department for Education and Skills (DfES) should appoint a family participation officer to promote family and community involvement in education and children's services provision.

Hargreaves (1994, cited in Harris, 2002) identified four *ideal types* of school culture (*formal, welfarist, hothouse and survivalist*) and argued that the culture most suited to an improving school was one that achieved a balance between academic pressure and social cohesion – usually a balance between the *welfarist* and *hothouse* cultures.

Such schools create an environment in which *for both teachers and students, school is a demanding but very enjoyable place to be* (Hargreaves, 1994, p11). As Harris (2002, p62) notes, *school improvement is essentially about constructing a better match between schools and young people. It is essentially about changing schools and, by definition, the patterns of relationships that exist between staff and students*.

If we are allowed to realistically see schools as places of social relationships and as locales for social inclusion – as well as vehicles for knowledge transfer and of output measurement – then the potential for service improvement based upon harnessing the skills and aptitudes of teachers, education welfare workers and social workers becomes all the more apparent.

School inclusion and disability

Whilst debates may continue to rage, there is real evidence that many children and young people with various forms of mobility needs, learning disabilities and sensory needs are accessing an education that would have been unheard of a few decades ago. There are huge strides still to be made, and the Inclusion Agenda does indeed often sit uncomfortably with the obsession with School Standards and Improving Performance Agenda, but social workers have a particular role to play as advocates within an evolving and dynamic system. Some time ago, Oliver (1983) identified the three roles for social workers in relation to disabled children and their families as being:

(1) the provision of emotional support;

(2) promoting access to relevant practical support; and

(3) attempting to reduce the negative impact of having to deal with discriminatory organisations and bureaucracies.

In terms of these expectations of social workers, we do not think much has changed in the
intervening decades since Oliver's statement. This is *what works* for families and their young
people and children, and this is what the practitioner should continue to offer. Parents want
access to flexible and responsive services, and young people themselves want workers to
focus on their wants and aspirations rather than their disabilities and impairments.

Paradoxically, whilst social work has, traditionally, been found guilty of paying too little
attention to the educational outcomes of children in public care, the same profession has,
at times, colluded in an overemphasis on *special education*, as if schooling is the location
for everything important, and local authorities (both education and social services) had
been quick to advocate residential special schools for disabled children, until budgetary
restrictions began to demand alternative provision.

As Corker (2000, p78) suggests: *With disabled children we forget about the informal part of
their lives, but I suspect that this is where most of their learning, both positive and negative,
takes place.* She further endorses the concept of *communities of practice* as a way of thinking about the circles of influence that surround any child (be they disabled or otherwise).

That said, the changing education landscape is always significant in terms of its dispropor-
tionate impact upon children with special educational needs, and their families. There is
some evidence (*Children Now*, 2006) that the much-vaunted academy schools contain
lower percentages of children with statements than the schools they replaced. Such *facts*
can mean different things: for example, it might indicate that selection is indeed taking
place and special educational needs children are being excluded, or it could indicate an
inclusive, progressive policy of de-registering children on the grounds of reducing labeling
and associated stigma. Either way, the move towards *independent State schools* (trust
schools) will lead to concerns about selection and a potential re-emergence of segregation
for disabled children.

Some campaigners would prefer to see special education renamed *segregated education*,
as a reflection of its true status and impact. In terms of a simplistic integration/segregation
fault line, those campaigning for integration appear to be gaining the upper hand. Since
1986 some 327 special schools have closed down, and some charities, such as Scope,
plan to close all of their schools by 2020. Nevertheless, some argue that a regime geared
to address particular needs – such as schooling for blind/visually impaired pupils or for
deaf/hearing impaired children and young people – has its proponents, advocates and
defenders.

We will finish this chapter with a lengthy but highly pertinent quotation, that best exemplifies the complex issues surrounding issues of special education and school inclusion policies:

Demands for inclusive schooling should concern not only the 'rights' of disabled children but are also part of a wider critique of that which constitutes itself as 'normal'. In the absence of such a critique, notions of 'opportunities' and 'rights' rest upon an understanding of 'normality' that reflects the partial self – interest of dominant social groups in our society. Our own starting point is that inclusive education is inextricably linked to a political critique of social values and practices and the structures and institutions that they support. The analysis of 'value' must explicate the role of education in the production and reproduction of different values, including the 'value' invested in children and young people as commodities and the representation of this value in terms of 'special' needs. In struggling for the implementation of inclusive practice we are engaging in a political process of transformation.
(Armstrong et al. 2000)

This book has been, explicitly, about the education and social work responses to specific groups of vulnerable children and young people – those not attending school, those excluded from school, those being educated elsewhere, those defined as having special needs, those who are looked after by the local authority – and in one sense these groups are not only separate, but every single child within each separate group is different and indeed unique. Yet in another sense, these children and young people are all one, but they are all outsiders. They all challenge the claim of the mainstream education system to be inclusive. They all hold up a mirror to our educational landscape and individually say *What's in there for me?*

Chapter 10
Pointers to the future?

We will have to rethink education and not simply 'improve' schools.
(Wigley, 2003, p183)

The true wealth of any society is simply its people. The real wealth creators are parents and teachers. Long term, everything else depends on them.
(Cardinal Basil Hume (quoted in Harris, 2002: frontispiece))

The second quote above merits some discussion. Basil Hume was asserting – as indeed have most social, political and religious leaders since the Enlightenment – that a nation's children are its future, that we depend upon their advancement, well-being and, increasingly, their capacity (as a dwindling number of potentially economically active adults) to generate sufficient wealth to support and care for an expanding number of older persons. So much we can agree upon, and what can be divined is that the current political orthodoxy is that the welfare of all citizens depends upon the educational experiences of all children, because, it is routinely asserted, *good education leads to good outcomes*.

In terms of the vision for education, children's services and care, there are some clearer indicators as to the immediate future, and then there are pointers towards the less well-charted middle distance. The implementation of *Every Child Matters* means that the emerging present is already known and mapped out: full service extended schools, wrap around care, the mass expansion of children's centres, children's services operating with *trust-like* arrangements, the continued fragmentation of generic social work and the re-positioning of child protection, child welfare, education welfare and childcare as a significant part of children's services in which *Education* is, inevitably, the senior partner. In terms of vision and an associated set of aspirations, the *aim is clearly to create greater alignment or integration of services to improve outcomes for children and young people and make sure they don't fall through the cracks between services* (King, 2006, p57).

But is it all going to work?

If history teaches anything (and educators should be best placed, one would hope, to learn from history) then it would appear that a small but significant percentage of the school age population has persistently and steadfastly refused to, or perhaps been unable to, conform to the exigencies of the State, whatever the sanctions devised by the regime of the day. In the quote at the beginning of Chapter 1, Sir Keith Joseph – one of the architects of social policy during the Conservative/Thatcher years – offers up a quasi-libertarian view of education as a form of tyranny, of indeed social control of those who do not want to be *schooled*. In a similar vein, some commentators have noted the progressive formalisation of schooling in the last decades of the twentieth century, mirroring the five features of formal learning as defined by Eraut (1994):

(1) a prescribed learning framework;

(2) an organised learning event or package;

(3) the presence of a designated teacher or trainer;

(4) the award of a qualification or credit;

(5) the external specification of outcome.

The assumption is that everyone can buy into this set of principles, that everyone will become stakeholders in the collective endeavour, and this assumption about the capacity (or wish) of everyone to *buy in* reveals the extent to which we are still a society bound by the ideas of modernity.

Indeed, the New Order for children's services can be conceptualised as being predicated upon five fundamental assumptions made by government about child welfare and well-being:

---

(1) All children need and want the same things (expressed as the five outcomes of the Children Act 2004).

(2) All families want their children to achieve these five outcomes, many of which are achieved through a partnership between families and the State, with the latter providing universal services such as education and health.

(3) Some families will need, and will ask for, additional help to keep their side of the bargain, and they should receive focused, targeted support (for example, from children's centres, Surestart, children's services' social workers, child and adolescent mental health services).

(4) However, some families will fail to keep their side of the bargain, by not sending their children to school, by not controlling their behaviour, by causing them significant harm. They thereby put themselves in the position of being involuntary clients (Trotter, 1999) and will thus require specialist services, many of which are underpinned by statutory requirements for intervention.

(5) All agencies can work together to provide seamless services if the organisational structures are correctly adjusted: historic problems are therefore managerial rather than theoretical or ideological.

Of course, there are other ways of thinking about the scenario:

(1) *All children need and want the same things (the five outcomes) – although they may be expressed differently.*

(2) *All families want their children to achieve these five outcomes, but some have different and diverse ways of thinking about how these outcomes might be attained. Some families and kinship groups may wish to work outside the family/State partnership, or may want the State to support different modes of provision to achieve the outcomes.*

(3) *Some families will need, and will indeed ask for, additional help to keep their side of the bargain, and they should receive focused, targeted support.*

(4) *Some families may appear to fail to keep their side of the bargain – by not sending their children to school, by not controlling their behaviour, by causing them significant harm – and thereby put themselves in the position of being* involuntary clients *(Trotter, 1999). But these are complex and contested notions, on which variations in the law (e.g. lowering the school leaving age, or allowing children to leave school and work) or variations in policy (e.g. rewarding schools for levels of social inclusion rather than qualification outputs) can have significant effects.*

(5) *Finally, all agencies can indeed work together to provide* seamless services *sometimes, but different professions bring different values and ideologies to the table, and this engenders creative and dynamic tensions – necessary in a post-modern working context. Change and progress comes about through the capacity for orthodoxies to be challenged, and thus diversity of opinion has be nurtured and encouraged.*

The old divide – between professions and between services

When writing nearly 20 years ago, Blyth and Milner (1987, p37) noted that *relationships between education and social services from central government down have been characterised by a signal failure to work together effectively*, and it is precisely this failure that has exercised the reforming zeal of the New Labour Government to address this problem. According to Miller (2005, p194) *it could be said that there exists a 'Great Divide' between formal and social education, and there is a case for increasing coordination both at the level of theory and practice, expanding the breadth of the education that we offer young people.* That much is relatively easy – the acknowledgement of past failures and a resolve to improve matters henceforth.

However, there remains the fundamental contradiction that will act as a powerful *driver* to sustain the Great Divide.

The 'New Great Divide' – between policy agendas

In terms of broad social policy objectives, Levitas (1998) identifies three discourses of social inclusion currently at work in New Labour thinking:

(1) a *redistributionist* discourse: which identifies poverty and economic disadvantage as the cause of exclusion;

(2) a *moral underclass* discourse: which sees social exclusion as the consequence of individual (and community) inadequacy; and

(3) a *social integrationist* discourse in which employability and labour market participation are the principal routes out of excluded status.

We can see that in terms of education (and social work) reforms, all three discourses are in operation. There are redistributionist attempts to reduce child poverty and to raise standards in schools across the country. The emphasis on school attendance and the prosecution of *defective* parents exemplifies the *moral underclass* discourse, and the emphasis on school achievement represents the *social integrationist* agenda.

Nevertheless, there is an inherent contradiction between the drive to raise standards and the imperative to promote school inclusion. Furthermore, there are potentially inherent contradictions between policy directives to loosen local education authority control over schools under the Education Bill and the exhortations to ensure social inclusion by making all schools genuinely accessible to all pupils.

Such a contradiction has been noted by Baroness Morris, now Chair of the new Children's Workforce Development Council, who commented about the 2006 Education White Paper (now the Education and Standards Bill):

> *It's a national shame that the State is such a bad parent. The White Paper acknowledges the educational needs of looked after children, which is fantastic ... but then proposes systems that will make it harder, not easier, to meet them. Those things happen when local authorities make them happen. The risk is that some heads won't make it happen. At the moment the White Paper isn't written in a way that will ensure somebody has the power to make it happen.*

In addition to fears that a loosened link between schools and local education authorities may lead to poor communication about children already in schools, concerns were expressed that the White Paper may enable schools to refuse entry to looked after children altogether (although this is now being addressed by the Government announcement, in March 2006, that children in care are guaranteed a place at a school of their choice, regardless of when they move and whether the school is full).

The future – for looked after children and young people?

Sir Bill Utting, former Chief Inspector of Social Services, when speaking at a conference entitled In Care and After (February 2006) stated that the lessons from the past reveal that *we must learn to do the simple things well*. Furthermore, he suggested that we must work within the context of the highest expectations, of believing that *standards for those formerly looked after should exceed the minimum* and that we need to recast our efforts within a *spirit of generosity*. Indeed, this *spirit of generosity* is required across the board in relation to the education of the most disadvantaged children and young people, as greater-than-average progress needs greater-than-average inputs (Heath, Colton and Aldgate, 1994).

At the same conference, Sonia Jackson hypothesised that if children looked after achieved the same education outcome levels as the average population, then the resulting reduction in secure estate costs (secure units, remand, prison) and in other associated activities (drugs and alcohol services, mental health services, probation and police time) could result in a saving of £16 billion per annum. Indeed, McParlin and Graham (1995, cited in Jackson 2001, p130) had noted that *care leavers make up 54% of the prison population aged under 25*, and thus it is advanced that substantial savings could be made if improved educational outcomes did indeed result in lower levels of offending behaviour and consequent imprisonment. However, it has been similarly asserted that such advances can only be achieved if the historic *dichotomy between care and education* (Jackson, 1983) is addressed.

According to Susannah Cheal (Chief Executive of the Who Cares? Trust – the national charity for children in residential or foster care): *Relationships between partners are most productive where there is a shared vision, a climate of trust, a willingness to co-operate and agreed terms of reference.*

The future – for all children?

The Government has established a set of six Public Service Agreement targets for all children, as follows:

(1) the 2003 total school absence rate to be reduced by 8 per cent (from 6.83 per cent to 6.28 per cent) by 2008. This equates to around 39,000 more pupils in school each day, and has been achieved, to date, by reducing the level of authorised absences;

(2) narrowing the gap in educational achievement between looked after children and their peers;

(3) raising standards of 11 year olds in English and Maths;

(4) raising standards of 14 year olds in English, Maths, ICT and Science;

(5) enhancing the take-up of sporting opportunities by 5 to 16 year olds; and

(6) 60 per cent of 16 year olds to achieve five GSCEs at grades A* to C by 2008, and all schools to have at least 30 per cent of pupils achieving this standard by 2008.

So, these are the objectives to be addressed by all agencies involved in the integrated children's services system, and they are therefore goals that should be motivating and driving the practice of all. No longer is it acceptable for practitioners to have *silo mind sets* leading to attitudes of *that's not my concern*. That said, it is unrealistic for teachers to necessarily see things as a social worker does – at one level their concerns are not the same – but at the very least the combined impact of research and the Quality Protects targets all serve to help the social worker recognise the importance of education for the most disadvantaged and excluded children and young people in our society, and help the teacher understand and acknowledge the impact of external concerns, threats ands risks on school behaviour and performance.

It has been suggested that if social work in Britain was to more closely identify with the European model of pedagogy (see Petrie, 2006), then the supposed *Great Divide* would be a little narrower, if nevertheless still there. Social work has slowly, belatedly and painfully learnt to appreciate the importance of education in the lives and life opportunities of their clients and service users. Within the context of contradictory messages from government, and the confusing mix of the *Every Child Matters*/Children Act agenda and *the Higher Standards, Better Schools for All*/Education Bill agenda, schools and teachers are also grappling with the purposes of education itself. As Miller (2005, p199) suggests, the process of *developing partnerships with social educators could point the way towards a more holistic and negotiable curriculum that engages more precisely with the needs of young people*. It could be in the milieu of social pedagogy and social education that social workers, education welfare officers, teachers and all of the other professions committed to the welfare of all children forge a new inclusive partnership that begins to address the historic divides between professionals, and the educational underachievement of so many children, young people and adults within our society. Let us hope so.

Appendix 1

Timeline of education and social work developments

1543		Legislation to prevent commoner women, artisans, labourers and servants from reading or discussing the Bible
1802	Factory Health and Morals Act	Restricted work in certain factories to 12 hours per day
1807	Samuel Whitbread's Poor Law Bill	Proposed that every child should have two years of education between the ages of 7 and 14
1833	Factory Act (extended in 1844 and 1867)	Imposed age restrictions on work in certain settings
1833		Public grants for elementary schooling
1839		Her Majesty's Inspectors of Schools first introduced
1844	Factory Act	Permitted children over the age of 8 to be employed halftime and those over 13 full time
1846		State sponsored teacher training scheme commenced
1869	National Education League	Campaign for universal and free elementary education
1870	(Forster's) Elementary Education Act	Set up elected school boards to establish schools funded by local rates, for 5 to 13 year olds
1874	Factory Act	Permitted children over 10 to be employed halftime and those over 14 full time
1880	Education Act	Compulsory education to the age of 10
1888	Local Government Act	Creation of county councils and county borough councils
1891		Abolition of fees for elementary education
1893	Elementary Education (Blind and Deaf Children) Act	
1893		Extension of school leaving age to 11
1899		Extension of school leaving age to 12; compulsory for school authorities to make provision for blind and deaf children up to age of 16
1902	(Balfour's) Education Act	Local authorities replaced school boards as responsible for schools
1906	Education (Provision of Meals) Act	Transfer of responsibility – from Poor Law to local education authorities – of discretionary provision of school meals for those in greatest need
1918	Education Act	Extension of school leaving age to 14; fees abolished in all elementary schools; shift of control to central government; local authorities reporting to central Board of Education

1926	Hadow Report	Recommended increasing school leaving age to 15 and selective education beginning at 11
1938	Spens Report	Recommended diversification of secondary provision
1943	Norwood Report	Recommended tripartite system – grammar; secondary modern; secondary technical
1944	(Butler's) Education Act	Compulsory and free State education from the age of 5–15, based upon a tripartite secondary system – *a national system, locally administered*
1954	Gurney-Dixon Report	
1959	Crowther Report	
1962	Education Act	Introduced mandatory grants to students undertaking undergraduate degrees
1963	Robbins Report	Expansion of higher education
1963	Newsom Report – *Half our Future*	Focus on underachieving secondary school pupils: *Intellectual talent is not a fixed quantity with which we have to work, but a variable that can be modified by social policy and educational approaches*
1967	Plowden Report *Children and their Primary Schools*	Focus on important role played by nursery provision in *areas of social deprivation*
1970	Education (Handicapped Children) Act	Transferred responsibility for education of children with learning disabilities from health services to local education authorities
1971	Education (Milk) Act	Removal of entitlement of free school milk for all children
1972		Minimum school leaving age raised from 15 to 16
1974	Ralphs Report	Defined the functions of education welfare services
1976	Education Act	Admissions to all State secondary schools should be non-selective
1978	Warnock Report – *Special Educational Needs*	Advocated integration of formerly segregated children into mainstream schools based upon addressing children's special educational needs
1981	Education (Special Education) Act	Integration of those with special educational needs via the *Statementing* process
1984	Police and Criminal Evidence Act	
1985	DfES White Paper *Better Schools*	Introduction of TCEI (Technical Vocational Education Initiative)
1986	Disabled Persons (Services, Consultation and Representation) Act	Social services must work with local education authorities to ensure appropriate assessment of disabled school leavers
1988	Education Reform Act	Creation of city technology colleges (CTCs) and grant-maintained or *opted-out* schools; diminution of local education authority powers and duties; LMS (Local Management of Schools); introduction of a National Curriculum (including for those with *special needs*); removal of polytechnics from local authority control
1989	Children Act	Including relevant sections on education supervision orders, children in need, children looked after
1992	DfES White Paper *Choice and Diversity: A New Framework for Schools*	Plans to expand CTCs, school specialisation

1992	Further and Higher Education Act	Unification of status and funding in higher education
1993	Education Act	Aim to increase grant-maintained sector. Local education authorities to assist schools in identifying any child who may have special educational needs and give additional support where needed
1995	DfES White Paper *Better Schools*	*it is vital that schools should always remember that preparation for working life is one of their principal functions*
1995	Disability Discrimination Act	
1996	Education Act	Legal framework for prosecutions: non-school attendance; school attendance orders
1997	White Paper Excellence in Schools	Core commitment to achieving *high standards for all: ... we must strive to eliminate, and never excuse, under-achievement in the most deprived parts of our country* (David Blunkett, Secretary of State for Education)
1998	Human Rights Act	
1998	School Standards and Framework Act	*duty on LEAs to promote high standards and produce Education Development Plans setting out key targets and how they will be met*
1998	Teaching and Higher Education Act	
1998	Protection of Young People Act	Codified rules regarding youth employment
2000	Children (Leaving Care) Act	
2000	Framework for the Assessment of Children in Need and their Families	Published by Department for Education and Skills, Department of Health, and Home Office
2000	Carers and Disabled Children Act	
2001	White Paper *Schools Achieving Success*	
2001	Special Educational Needs and Disability Act (SENDA)	Part I: *All children with statements must be educated in mainstream school unless this would be detrimental to the efficient education of other children, or against parental wishes.* Schools required to make *reasonable adjustments* to ensure disabled children are not disadvantaged
2002	Education Act	Focus on specialist schools; Beacon schools; promotion of *faith-based schools*
2003	Anti-social Behaviour Act	
2004	Children Act	Enacting recommendations of the Laming Report *Every Child Matters*, related to the Climbié Inquiry, and government strategy via *Every Child Matters: Change for Children*
2005	*Youth Matters*	Parallel document for young people: integrating *Connexions* into local authorities
	Education White Paper *Higher Standards, Better Schools For All*	
2006	Education and Inspection Bill	Determining degree of independence for schools in terms of admissions policies and procedures
2006	Childcare Bill	Places a duty on local authorities to meet the needs of working parents. Rights to accessible high quality childcare
2006	Safeguarding Vulnerable Groups Bill	
2006	Youth Justice Bill	

Appendix 2
Identifying barriers to access: A checklist

How does your school deliver the curriculum?

QUESTION	YES	NO
Do you ensure that teachers and teaching assistants have the necessary training to teach and support disabled pupils?		
Are your classrooms optimally organised for disabled pupils?		
Do lessons provide opportunities for all pupils to achieve?		
Are lessons responsive to pupil diversity?		
Do lessons involve work to be done by individuals, pairs, groups and the whole class?		
Are all pupils encouraged to take part in music, drama and physical activities?		
Do staff recognise and allow for the mental effort expended by some disabled pupils, for example using lip reading?		
Do staff provide alternative ways of giving access to experience or understanding for disabled pupils who cannot engage in particular activities, for example some form of exercise in physical education?		
Do you provide access to computer technology appropriate for students with disabilities?		
Are school visits, including overseas visits, made accessible to all pupils irrespective of attainment or impairment?		
Are there high expectations of all pupils?		
Do the staff seek to remove all barriers to learning and participation?		

Source: DfES (2002) *Accessible Schools: Summary Guidance*

Appendix 3
Resources and information

HOME EDUCATION	
Department for Education and Skills (DfES) Elective Home Education GF D Mowden Hall County Durham DL3 9BJ Tel: 01325 391 186	Home Education Advisory Service PO Box 98 Welwyn Garden City Hertfordshire AL8 6AN Tel: 01707 371 854
Education Otherwise PO Box 7420 London N9 9SG Tel: 01283 532 547	
INCLUSIVE EDUCATION	
The Centre for Studies on Inclusive Education (CSIE) New Redland Frenchay Campus Coldharbour Lane Bristol BS16 1QU Tel: 0113 243 0202	CHANGE Unity Business Centre Units 19 and 20, 26 Roundhay Road Leeds LS7 1AB Tel: 0117 344 4007
The National Association for Special Educational Needs (NASEN) NASEN House 4/5 Amber Business Village Amber Close Arnington Tamworth B77 4RP Tel: 01827 311 500	The Council for Disabled Children **www.ncb.org.uk/cdc** Tel: 0207 843 6045
The Children's Trust Tadworth Court Tadworth Surrey KT20 5RU Tel: 01737 365 000	

CHILDREN'S ORGANISATIONS	
The Confederation of Education and Children's Services Managers (ConfEd) **www.confed.org.uk**	
Voice for the Child in Care Unit 4 Pride Court 80–82 White Lion Street London N1 9PF **www.vcc-uk.org**	The Who Cares? Trust Kemp House 152–160 City Road London EC1V 2NP **www.thewhocarestrust.org.uk**

References

Allen-Meares, P, Washington, R and Welsh, B (2000) *Social work services in schools*. 3rd edition. Needham Heights, MA: Allyn and Bacon.

Anderson, E (2005) *Residential and boarding education and care for young people*. London: Routledge, Taylor and Francis Group.

Armstrong, D, Armstrong, F and Barton, L (eds) (2000) *Inclusive education: Policy, contexts and comparative perspectives*. London: David Fulton.

Atkinson, M, Halsey, K, Wilkin, A and Kinder, K (2000) *Raising attendance: working practices and current initiatives within the education welfare service*. Slough: NFER.

Audit Commission (1994) *Seen But Not Heard: Coordinating Child Health and Social Services for Children in Need*. London: The Stationery Office.

Audit Commission (1996) *Misspent Youth – Young People and Crime*. London: The Audit Commission

Bagley, C and Pritchard, C (1998) 'Problem Behaviours and School Exclusion in At-risk Youth', *Child and Family Social Work*, November 1998, Vol 3, Issue 4, pp219–226.

Beckett, C (2006) *Essential theory for social work practice*. London: Sage.

Bell, M and Wilson, K (eds) (2003) *The practitioner's guide to working with families*. Basingstoke: Palgrave Macmillan.

Benn, M (2005) 'We Need Fairness on Schools, Not Choice', *Community Care*, 13–19 October 2005.

Bentley, T and Gurumurthy, R (1999) *Destination unknown: Engaging with the problems of marginalised youth*. London: Demos.

Beresford, P (1994) *Positively parents: Caring for a severely disabled child*. London: The Stationery Office/ CCETSW.

Berridge, D and Brodie, I (1998) *Children's home revisited*. London: Jessica Kingsley.

Blair, T (1996) *New Britain: My vision of a young country*. London: Fourth Estate.

Blair, T (2004) *Fabian Lecture on Education at the Institute of Education, Wednesday 7 July*, available at: **www.suttontrust.com**.

Blyth, E (2000) 'Education Social Work', in M. Davies (ed) *The Blackwell dictionary of social work*. Oxford: Blackwell.

Blyth, E and Milner, J (1987) 'Running a Viable Education Welfare Option on a CQSW course', *Issues in Social Work Education*, 7: 1.

Blyth, E and Milner, J (1993) 'Exclusion from School: a First Step in Exclusion from Society?' *Children and Society*, 7: 3.

Blyth, E and Milner, J (1996) *Exclusion from school: Inter-professional issues, policy and practice*. London: Routledge.

Blyth, E and Milner, J (1997) *Social work with children: The educational perspective*. London: Longman.

Blyth, E and Milner, J (eds) (1999) *Improving school attendance*. London: Routledge.

Booth, T (1983) 'Policies Towards the Integration of Mentally Handicapped Children in Education', *Oxford Review of Education*, Vol 9, No 39, pp255–68.

Boyson, R (1975) *The crisis in education*. London: Woburn.

Brannen, J and Moss, P (eds) (2003) *Rethinking childcare*. Buckingham: Open University.

Brayne, H and Carr, H (2005) *Law for social workers*, 9th edition. Oxford: Oxford University Press.

Brodie, I (2001) *Children's homes and school exclusion*. London: Jessica Kingsley.

Byrne, D (1999) *Social exclusion*. Buckingham: Open University Press.

Calder, M and Hackett, S (2003) *Assessment in Child Care* Lyme Regis: Russell House Publishing

Calman, T (2001) 'Special Educational Needs', in L.A. Cull and J. Roche (eds) *The law and social work*. Basingstoke: Palgrave.

CCETSW (1992) *Preparing for Work in the Education Welfare Service: Improving Social Work Education and Training*, No 13. London: CCETSW.

Central Advisory Council for Education (1967) *Children and their Primary Schools* (Plowden Report). London: The Stationery Office.

Centre for Studies on Inclusive Education (2005*) Segregation Trends – LEAs in England 2002–04*.

Chase, E, Simon, A and Jackson, S (eds) (2006) *In care and after: A positive perspective*. Abingdon: Routledge.

Cherry, S (2005) *Transforming behaviour: Pro-social modelling in practice*. Cullompton: Willan Publishing.

Chief Secretary to the Treasury (2003) *Every Child Matters* (Cm 5860). London: Stationery Office.

Chitty, C (2004) *Education policy in Britain*. Basingstoke: Palgrave.

Clough, P and Corbett, J (ed) (2000) *Theories of inclusive education*. London: Paul Chapman Publishing.

Cohen, S (1972) *Folk devils and moral panics*. Oxford: Martin Robertson.

Corrigan, P (1977*) Schooling the smash street kids*. London: Macmillan.

Cullingford, C (1999) *The causes of exclusion: Home, school and the development of young criminals*. London: Kogan Page.

Cunningham, H (1995) *Children and childhood in western society since 1500*. Harlow: Longman.

CYPU (Children and Young People's Unit) (2001) *Building a Strategy for Children and Young People: A Consultation Document*. London: CYPU.

Davin, A (1996) *Growing Up Poor* London: Rivers Oram Press.

Department for Education and Science (1984) *The Education Welfare Service: Report by Her Majesty's Inspectorate*. London: The Stationery Office.

Department for Education and Science (1986) *School Attendance and Education Welfare Services* Circular 2/86.

Department for Education (1994) *School Attendance: Policy and Practice on Categorisation of Absence*. London: The Stationery Office.

Department for Education and Employment (1998) *Disaffected Children*. London: DfEE.

Department for Education and Employment (1999) *Social Inclusion: Pupil Support – The Secretary of State's Guidance on Pupil Attendance, Behaviour, Exclusion and Re-Integration* Circular No 10/99. London: DfEE/Social Exclusion Unit/ Home Office/Department of Health.

Department for Education and Employment/Department of Health (2000) *Guidance on the Education of Children and Young People in Public Care* Circular 2000 (13). London: DfEE/ DoH.

Department for Education and Skills (2000) *Schools: Building upon Success*. London: DfES.

Department for Education and Skills (2002a) *Accessible Schools: Planning to Increase Access to Schools for Disabled Pupils*.

Department for Education and Skills (2002b) *Truancy Sweeps, Information and Data-Sharing*. London: DfES.

Department for Education and Skills (2003a) Pupil Absence in Schools in England 2002–03.

Department for Education and Skills (2003b) *Pupil Characteristics and Class Sizes in Maintained Schools in England, January 2003*. London: Stationery Office.

Department for Education and Skills (2003c) *Permanent Exclusions from Schools and Exclusion Appeals, England 2001–02*. London: Stationery Office.

Department for Education and Skills (2003d) *Ensuring Regular School Attendance: Guidance on the Legal Measures available to Secure Regular School Attendance*. London: Stationery Office.

Department for Education and Skills (2003e) *Ensuring Regular School Attendance* Nottingham: DfES Publications.

Department for Education and Skills (2004a) *Absence from School: A Study of its Causes and Effects in Seven LEAs*, available at: **www.dfes.gov.uk/research/data/uploadfiles/RR424.pdf.**

Department for Education and Skills (2004b) *Guidance on Education-related Parenting Contracts, Parenting Orders and Penalty Notices*. Nottingham: DfES Publications.

Department for Education and Skills (2004c) *Building a Children's Workforce – Common Core of Skills and Knowledge for the Children's Workforce*. Nottingham: DfES Publications.

Department for Education and Skills (2004d) *Removing Barriers to Achievement* Nottingham: DfES Publications.

Department for Education and Skills (2005a), see: **www.everychildmatters.gov.uk/ete/welfare/.**

Department for Education and Skills (2005b), see: **www.everychildmatters.gov.uk/socialcare/ disabledchildren/facts/.**

Department for Education and Skills (2005c) *Higher Standards: Better Schools for All.*

Department for Education and Skills (2005d) *Children Looked After by Local Authorities, Year Ending 31st March 2004.* London: DfES.

Department for Education and Skills (2005e) *Statistics of Education: Children Looked After in England 2003–2004.* London: DfES.

Department of Health (1991) *Patterns and Outcomes.* London: The Stationery Office.

Department of Health (1996) *Focus on Teenagers: Messages from Research.* London: The Stationery Office.

Department of Health (1998a) *Quality Protects: Transforming Children's Services.* London: The Stationery Office.

Department of Health (1998b) *Modernising Social Services.* London: The Stationery Office.

Department of Health (1998c) *Caring for children looked after away from home.* Chichester: Wiley Publishing.

Department of Health (1999) *Working Together to Safeguard Children. A Guide to Inter-agency Working to Safeguard and Promote the Welfare of Children.* London: The Stationery Office.

Department of Health (2001) *Valuing People: A New Strategy for Learning Disability for the 21st Century.* London: The Stationery Office.

Department of Health/Department for Education and Skills/Home Office (2000) *The Framework for the Assessment of Children in Need and their Families.* London: The Stationery Office.

Department of Health and Home Office (2003) *The Victoria Climbié Inquiry: Report of an Inquiry by Lord Laming.* London: Stationery Office.

Dixon, B (2004) *Education – a social worker's handbook.* Manchester: National Teachers Advisory Service.

Douglas, JWB (1964) *The home and the school.* London: MacGibbon and Kee.

Dyson, A (2002) 'Inclusive Education', in D. McNeish, T. Newman, and H. Roberts (eds) *What works for children?.* Buckingham: Open University Press.

Eraut, M (1994) *Developing professional knowledge and competence.* London: Falmer Press.

Farrington, D (1995) 'The Development of Offending and Anti-social Behaviour from Childhood', in *Journal of Child Psychology and Psychiatry*, 36, pp929–64.

Farrington, D (1996) 'Later Life Outcomes of Truants in the Cambridge Study', in I. Berg, and J. Nursten, (eds) *Unwillingly to school.* Gaskell.

Fawcett, B, Featherstone, B and Goddard, J (2004) *Contemporary childcare policy and practice.* Basingstoke: Palgrave.

Firth, H and Fletcher, B (2001) 'Developing Equal Chances: A Whole Authority Approach', in S. Jackson (ed) *Nobody ever told us school mattered.* London: BAAF.

Fitzherbert, K (1977) *Childcare services and the teacher.* London: Temple Smith.

Fletcher-Campbell, F and Hall, C (1990) *The education of children in care*. Slough: NFER.

Fletcher-Campbell, F (1997) *The education of children who are looked after*. Slough: NFER.

Fox Harding, L (1997) *Perspectives in childcare policy*, 2nd edition. Harlow: Longman.

Francis, J (2000) 'Investing in Children's Futures: Enhancing the Educational Arrangements of 'Looked After' Children and Young People', *Child and Family Social Work*, 5 (1), pp23–33.

Frank, J, Tatum, C and Tucker, S (1999) *On small shoulders: Learning from the experiences of former young carers*. London: The Children's Society.

Fullan, M (1999) *Change forces – the sequel*. London: Falmer.

Gallagher, Brannan, C, Jones, R and Westwood, S (2004) 'Good Practice in the Education of Children in Residential Care', *British Journal of Social Work*, 34, pp1133–1160.

General Social Care Council (2002) *Codes of Practice for Social Care Workers and Employers*. London: General Social Care Council.

General Teaching Council (2002) *The Code of Professional Values and Practice for Teachers*. London: GTC.

Gilligan, R (1998) 'The Importance of Schools and Teachers in Child Welfare', *Child and Family Social Work*, **3** (1), pp13–25.

Gittins, D (1998) *The child in question*. Basingstoke: Macmillan.

Godwin, W (1793) 'The Evils of National Education', in G. Woodcock (ed) (1977) *The anarchist reader*. London: Fontana.

Goldson, B (ed) (2000) *The new youth justice*. Lyme Regis: Russell House Publishing.

Goldson, B (2003) *Vulnerable inside: Children in secure and penal settings*. London: The Children's Society.

Goldson, B (2004) 'Victims or Threats? Children, Care and Control', in J. Fink (ed) *Care: Personal lives and social policy*. Bristol: The Policy Press.

Goldson, B, Lavalette, M and McKecknie, J (eds) (2002) *Children, welfare and the state*. London: Sage.

Graham, J and Bowling, B (1995) *Young People and Crime: Home Office Research Study 145*. London: Home Office.

Grier, A and Thomas, T (2005) 'Troubled and in Trouble: Young People, Truancy and Offending', in R. Adams, L. Dominelli and M. Payne (eds) *Social work futures*. Basingstoke: Palgrave Macmillan.

Halsey, K, Johnson, A, Kinder, K and Fletcher-Morgan, C (2003) *Evaluation of truancy sweep follow-ups*. Nottingham: NFER/ DfES.

Hargreaves, A (1994) *Changing teachers, changing times*. London: Cassell.

Harris A (2002) *School improvement: What's in it for schools?*. London: Routledge Falmer.

Harrison, R and Wise, C (eds) (2005) *Working with young people*. London: Sage.

Hayden, C (1997) *Children excluded from primary school: Debates, evidence, responses*. Buckingham: Open University Press.

Hayden C and Dunne S (2001) *Outside looking in: Children and families' experience of school exclusion*. London: The Children's Society.

Heath, A, Colton, M and Aldgate, J (1994) 'Failure to Escape: A Longitudinal Study of Foster Children's Educational Attainment', *British Journal of Social Work*, **24 (3)**, pp241–60.

Hendrick, H (2003) *Child welfare: Historical dimensions, contemporary debate*. Bristol: Polity Press.

Herbert, C (1996) *Stop the bullying*. C Herbert Publishing.

Herbert, M (2002) ' The Human Life Cycle: Adolescence' in M. Davies (ed) *Companion to social work*, 2nd edition. Oxford: Blackwell.

Hill, M (2004) *Understanding social policy*, 7th edition. Oxford: Blackwell.

Holland, P (1992) *What is a child? Popular images of childhood*. London: Virago.

Holman, B (2004) 'Undo the Wrapping', *Community Care*, 21–27 October 2004.

Home Office (1997) *No More Excuses*, White Paper. London: Stationery Office.

Home Office (2003) *Home Office Research Study 268: Vulnerability and Involvement in Drug Use and Sex Work*.

Hopkins–Burke, R (2001) *An introduction to criminological theory*. Devon: Willan Publishing.

Horner, N (2006) *What is social work? Context and perspectives*, 2nd edition. Exeter: Learning Matters.

Hoyle, D (1998) 'Constructions of Pupil Absence in the British Education Service', *Child and Family Social Work*, **3** (2), pp99–111.

Hudson, B (2005) 'What's The Plan?', *Community Care*, 3–9th November, pp36–37.

Hughes, J (2005) 'Specific Areas of Practice with Children and Families: Children with Disabilities', in M. Jowitt and S. O'Loughlin (eds) *Social work with children and families*. Exeter: Learning Matters.

Hunt, T (2004) *Building Jerusalem*. London: Weidenfeld and Nicholson.

Huxtable, M and Blyth, E (eds) (2000) *School social work worldwide*. Washington, DC: National Association of Social Work.

Hyams-Parish, T (1995) *Banished to the exclusion zone – a guide to school exclusions and the law*. London: Children's Legal Centre.

Illich, I (1970) *Deschooling society*. New York: Harper and Row.

Jackson, S (1983) *The Education of Children in Care: Report to the Social Services Research Council* (unpublished).

Jackson, S (1994) 'Educating Children in Residential and Foster Care', *Oxford Review of Education*, **20**, pp267–79.

Jackson, S (ed) (2001) *Nobody ever told us school mattered*. London: BAAF.

Jackson, S (2002) 'Promoting Stability and Continuity in Care Away From Home', in D. McNeish, T. Newman, and H. Roberts (eds) *What works for children?* Buckingham: Open University Press.

Jackson, S and McParlin, P (2006) 'The Education of Children in Care', *The Psychologist*, Vol 19, No 2, pp90–93.

Jackson, S and Sachdev, D (2001) *Better education, better futures: Research, practice and the views of young people in public care*. Ilford: Barnardo's.

Jackson, S and Simon, A (2005) 'The Costs and Benefits of Educating Children in Care', in E. Chase, A. Simon and S. Jackson (eds) *In care and after: A positive perspective*. London: Routledge.

Jackson, S, Ajayi, S and Quigley, M (2003) *By degrees: The first year – from care to university*. London: National Children's Bureau/ The Frank Buttle Trust.

Jeffs, T and Smith, M (2002) 'Social Exclusion, Joined Up Thinking and Individualization – New Labour's Connexions Strategy', available at: **www.Infed.org**.

Johns, R (2005) *Using the law in social work*, 2nd edition. Exeter: Learning Matters.

Johnstone, Munn and Edwards (1992) *Action Against Bullying: A Support Pack for Schools*. Scottish Council for Research in Education.

Joseph Rowntree Foundation (2003) *Factors that Influence Young People Leaving Care*.

Juby, H and Farrington, D (2001) 'Disentangling the Link between Family Disruption and Delinquency', *British Journal of Criminology*, 41, pp22–40.

Kendall, S, White, R, and Kinder, K (2003) *School attendance and the prosecution of parents: Perspectives from education welfare service management*. Slough: NFER.

Kendall, S, White, R, Kinder, K, Halsey, K and Bedford, N (2004) *School attendance and the prosecution of parents: Effects and effectiveness*. Slough: NFER.

Kinder, K, Atkinson, M, Wilkin, A and Bruce, D (2001) *The role of the LEA in reducing truancy*. York: NFER.

King, A (2006) 'How Integrated Services for Children will affect the Teaching Profession', *Education Review*, Vol 18, No 2, pp56–62.

Levitas R (1998) *The inclusive society? Social exclusion and New Labour*. London: Macmillan.

Link, R (1982) 'Before the Bell Tolls', *Social Work Today*, **13**, p31.

Local Government Training Board (1974) *Report of the Working Party on the Role and Training of Education Welfare Officers* (Ralphs Report). London: The Stationery Office.

London Borough of Brent (2005) *Education Welfare Service*.

Lovering, K and Caldwell, A (2003) *Scallywags: Interagency Early Intervention Project for Children with Emotional and Behavioural Problems*. Exeter: Centre for Evidence Based Social Services (cf: **www.ex.ac.uk/files/scallywags.pdf**).

Lyons, K (2002) 'Social Work and Schools' in M Davies (ed) *Companion to Social Work* 2nd edition. Oxford: Blackwell.

MacDonald, M and Daly, B (eds) (1996) *Enhancing Attendance: A Teacher's Guide to Improving School Attendance*. Northumberland County Council.

Madelson, P and Liddle, R (1996) *The Blair revolution: Can New Labour deliver?* London: Faber and Faber.

Maguire, M, Morgan, R and Reiner, R (eds) (2000) *The Oxford handbook of criminology*, 3rd edition. Oxford: Oxford University Press.

Maitles, H (2002) 'Children and Education: Inequalities in Our Schools', in B. Goldson, M. Lavalette, and J. McKecknie (eds) (2002) *Children, Welfare and the State*. London: Sage.

Mandeville, B (1970) *The fable of the bees*. Harmondsworth: Penguin.

Martin, P and Jackson, S (2002) 'Educational Success for Children in Public Care: Advice from a Group of High Achievers', *Child and Family Social Work*, 7 (2), pp121–130.

Mayhew, E, Finch, N, Beresford B and Keung A (2005) 'Children's Time and Space', in J. Bradshaw and E. Mayhew (eds) *The well being of children in the UK*. London: Save the Children Fund.

McNeish, D, Newman, T and Roberts, H (2002) *What works for children?* Buckingham: Open University Press.

McParlin, P and Graham, E (1995) 'Time to Care about those in Care', *Times Higher Education Supplement*, 13 October 1995.

Measham, F and Paylor, I (2005) 'Legal and Illicit Drug Use', in R. Adams, L. Dominelli and M. Payne (eds) *Social work futures*. Basingstoke: Palgrave Macmillan.

Miller, J, Flood-Page, C, Campbell, S and Harrington (1999) *Home Office Research Study 209: Youth Crime: Findings from the 1998/99 Youth Lifestyles Survey*.

Miller, T (2005) 'Across the Great Divide: Creating Partnerships in Education', in R. Carnwell and J. Buchanan (eds) *Effective practice in health and social care: A partnership approach*. Maidenhead: Open University Press.

Miller, W (1983) 'Motivational Interviewing with Problem Drinkers', *Behavioural Psychology, (11)*.

Mittler, P (2000) *Working towards inclusive education*. London: David Fulton.

Mizen, P (2003) 'The Best Days of Your Life? Youth, Policy and Blair's New Labour', *Critical Social Policy*, 23 (4), pp453–476.

Mizen, P (2004) *The changing state of youth*. Basingstoke: Palgrave Macmillan.

Muncie, J (2004) *Youth and crime*, 2nd edition. London: Sage.

Munn, P, Lloyd, G and Cullen, MA (2000) *Alternatives to exclusion from school*. London: Paul Chapman Publishing.

National Audit Office (2005) *Improving School Attendance in England*.

National Children's Home (2005) *Close the Gap for Children in Care*.

Newburn, T and Shiner, M (2005) *Dealing with disaffection: Young people, mentoring and social inclusion*. Devon: Willan Publishing.

Office for National Statistics (2003) *Social Trends 33*. London: The Stationery Office.

O'Keefe, D (1994) *Truancy in English Secondary Schools*. London: The Stationery Office.

Oliver, C and Candappa, M (2003) *Tackling Bullying: Listening to the Views of Children and Young People*. London: Thomas Coram Research Unit/Institute of Education.

Oliver, M (1996) *Understanding disability: From theory to practice*. Basingstoke: Macmillan.

Parker, J and Bradley, G (2003) *Assessment, planning, intervention and review* Exeter: Learning Matters.

Parsons, C and Howlett, K (2000) *Investigating the reintegration of permanently excluded pupils in England*. Sheffield: CSNU.

Parsons, C, Godfrey, R, Howlett, K and Martin, T (2001*) Outcomes in secondary education for children excluded from primary school*. London: DfES.

Parton, N (2006) *Safeguarding childhood*. Basingstoke: Palgrave Macmillan.

Pearce, N and Hillman, J (1998) *Wasted Youth: Raising Achievement and Tackling Social Exclusion*. London: Institute for Public Policy Research.

Pearson, G (1983) *Hooligan: A history of respectable fears*. Basingstoke: Macmillan.

Petrie, P (2003) 'Social Pedagogy', in J. Brannen and P. Moss (eds) *Rethinking children's care*. Buckingham: Open University Press.

Pierson, J (2002) *Tackling social exclusion*. London: Routledge.

Prochaska, J, DiClemente, C and Norcross, J (1994) *Changing for good*. New York: Avon Books.

Quinney, A (2006) *Collaborative social work practice*. Exeter: Learning Matters.

Reid, K (1986) *Disaffection from school*. London: Methuen.

Reid, K (2000) *Tackling truancy in schools: A practical manual for primary and secondary schools*. London: Routledge.

Reid, K (2002) *Truancy*. London: Routledge Falmer.

Reid, K (2003) 'The Search for Solutions to Truancy and Other Forms of School Absenteeism', *Pastoral Care*, March 2003.

Roche, J (2004) *Youth in society: Contemporary theory, policy and practice*. London: Sage.

Rothermel, P (2002) *Home Education: Rationales, Practices and Outcomes* (available at: **www.dur.ac.uk/p.j.rothermel/Research/Researchpaper/BERAworkingpaper.htm**).

Sasson (1993) 'The Price of Banishment', *Education*, 181 (6), p111.

Save the Children (2003) *Missing out on education*. London: Save the Children.

Seden, J (1999) *Counselling skills in social work practice*. Buckingham: Open University Press.

Seebohm Report (1968) *Report of the Committee on Local Authority and Allied Personal Social Services*, Cmnd.3703. London: The Stationery Office.

Shakespeare, T (2000) *Help*. Birmingham: Venture Press/BASW.

Sinclair, I and Gibbs, I (1998) *Children's homes: A study in diversity*. Chichester: Wiley.

Smith, R (2003) *Youth justice: Ideas, policy, practice*. Devon: Willan Publishing.

Social Exclusion Unit (1998) *Truancy and School Exclusion*. London: Cabinet Office.

Social Exclusion Unit (1999) *Bridging the Gap: New Opportunities for 16–18 year olds not in Education, Employment or Training*. London: The Stationery Office.

Social Exclusion Unit (2001) *Preventing School Exclusion*. London: Cabinet Office.

Social Exclusion Unit (2003) *A Better Education for Children in Care*. London: The Stationery Office.

Society Guardian, with NCH (2003) *Working with Children 2004 –05*. London: Guardian Books.

Society Guardian, with NCH (2005) *Working with Children 2006–07*. London: Guardian Books.

Stack, N and McKechnie, J (2002) 'Working Children', in B. Goldson, M. Lavalette and J. McKecknie (eds) *Children, welfare and the State*. London: Sage.

Stein, M (1997) *What works in leaving care? – Summary*. Barnardo's.

Stepney, P and Ford, D (eds) (2000) *Social work models, methods and theories*. Lyme Regis: Russell House Publishing.

Strachey, L (1986) *Eminent Victorians*. London: Penguin.

Support force for Residential Child Care (1996) Good care matters: Ways of enhancing good practice in residential child care. London: DoH.

Tawney, RH (1931) *Equality*. London: Unwin Books.

Teacher Training Agency (2005) *Handbook of Guidance*. Available from: **www.tda.gov.uk**

The Guardian (2005) 'MPs say £885m wasted on bid to cut truancy', 20 January 2005.

Thrupp, M (1999) *School improvement: Let's be realistic*. London: Falmer Press.

Toynbee, P and Walker, P (2001) *Did things get better? An audit of Labour's successes and failures*. London: Penguin.

Trevithick, P (2000) *Social work skills – A practice handbook*. Buckingham: Open University Press.

Trotter, C (1999) *Working with involuntary clients*. London: Sage.

Trowler, R (1998) *Education policy*. Eastbourne: The Gildredge Press.

TUC/MORI Poll (2001) *Half a Million Kids Working Illegally*, TUC Report, 21 March 2001.

Utting, Sir, W (1997) *People Like Us*. London: The Stationery Office.

Valio, N (2005) 'Exams? Pass on that one', *Community Care*, 1–7 September 2005.

Walker, S and Beckett, C (2003) *Social work assessment and intervention*. Lyme Regis: Russell House Publishing.

Warnock, M (1980) 'A flexible framework', *The Times Educational Supplement*, 26 September 1980.

Welshman, J (1999) 'The Social History of Social Work: The Issue of 'The Problem Family' 1940–70', *British Journal of Social Work*, **29** (3), pp457–76.

Whalley, M (2001) *Involving parents in their children's learning*. London: Paul Chapman Publishing.

Wheal, A (2004) *Adolescence*, 2nd edition. Lyme Regis: Russell House Publishing.

Wheatley, H (2005) 'Caring After Hours', *Community Care*, 1–7 September 2005.

Whitaker, D, Archer, L and Hicks, L (1998) *Working in children's homes: Challenges and complexities*. Chichester: Wiley.

Whitney, B (1998) 'Child Employment Legislation: Changing the Focus', in B. Petit (ed) *Children and work in the UK: Reassessing the issues*. London: Child Poverty Action Group.

Whitty, G (2002) *Making sense of education policy*. London: Paul Chapman Publishing.

Wilsher, A (1999) 'Can Do!', *Nursery World*, 99, p21.

Work Smart (2003) Children's Work Rights, available at: **www.worksmart.org.uk/rights/viewsubsection**.

Wright, C, Weeks, D and McGlaughlin, A (2000) *Race, class and gender in exclusion from school*. London: Falmer Press.

Wrigley, T (2003) *Schools of hope*. Stoke on Trent: Trentham Books.

Youth Justice Board (2003a) *Reader: Education, training and employment (community)*. London: ECOTEC.

Youth Justice Board (2003b) *Youth Justice Board for England and Wales Corporate Plan 2003–04 to 2005–06*. London: Youth Justice Board.

Youth Justice Board: *Key Elements of Effective Practice*, available at: **www.youth-justice-board-gov.uk/publications/Scripts**.

Index

Added to a page number 't' denotes a table.